LONE EAGLE

THE FIGHTER PILOT EXPERIENCE

PHILIP KAPLAN

Skyhorse Publishing books may be purchased in bulk at special discounts for sales promotion, corporate gifts, fund-raising, or educational purposes. Special editions can also be created to specifications. For details, contact the Special Sales Department, Skyhorse Publishing, 307 West 36th Street, 11th Floor, New York, NY 10018 or info@skyhorsepublishing.com.

Skyhorse® and Skyhorse Publishing ® are registered trademarks of Skyhorse Publishing, Inc.®, a Delaware corporation.

Visit our website at www.skyhorsepublishing.com.

10 9 8 7 6 5 4 3 2 1

Library of Congress Cataloging-in-Publication Data is available on file.

Cover design by Rain Saukas
Cover photographs courtesy of Philip Kaplan

Adapted from *Fighter Pilot*

Print ISBN: 978-1-51070-511-1
Ebook ISBN: 978-1-51070-516-6

Printed in China

CONTENTS

FLEDGLINGS

". . . the First World War . . . took me from school at sixteen, it destroyed all hope of University training or apprenticeship to a trade, it deprived me of the only carefree years, and washed me up, inequipped for any serious career, with a Military Cross, a Royal handshake, a six-hundred-pound gratuity, and—I almost forgot to say—my life. There were men older than I whose education was complete. To them the War was a setback, disastrous but not irremediable. There were others, older still, who had positions to which they could return. But we very young men had no place, actual or prospective, in a peaceful world. We walked off the playing-fields into the lines. Our preoccupation was the next patrol, or horizon the next leave. We were trained with one object—to kill. We had one hope—to live. When it was over we had to start again."
—from *Sagittarius Rising* by Cecil Lewis

"Mark Twain said, 'Courage is the mastery of fear, resistance to fear, not the absence of fear.' At times the nearness of death brings an inexplicable exhilaration which starts the adrenaline flowing and results in instant action. The plane becomes an integral part of the pilot's body, it is strapped to his butt, and they become a single fighting machine."
—from *Double Nickel-Double Trouble* by R. M. Littlefield

HE CAME FROM JAVA, the son of a wealthy Dutch coffee planter. The family returned to the Netherlands in 1897 when he was six, so that he could be educated there. Little

Antony Fokker was reputed to be spoiled, cocky, arrogant, and selfish, as well as extremely bright and inventive.

He became interested in aviation at an automobile and airplane exhibition in Brussels, but was not encouraged by his father. Hermann Fokker told the boy that he would never buy him an airplane, believing, as did so many in the early part of the century, that one must have a death wish to get involved with flying machines.

For all his protestations, Hermann Fokker kept his son, now enrolled in an aeronautical engineering school, well-financed through the boy's first attempts to build a successful flying machine. The elder Fokker provided more than 180,000 marks to keep his son afloat in his continuous failures, and was astonished when, early in World War I, young Antony was able to repay his father every cent, with interest.

In the year leading up to that war, Antony Fokker followed the principles of automatic stability that he had developed as a child building experimental model airplanes and concentrated on the design and construction of a series of planes that he called *Spinne* (Spider). These were a simple blend of skids with wheels attached, tilted fabric-covered wings, and welded tubes, wires, and turnbuckles . . . all improvised into forms and shapes from his wild imagination. He dedicated himself to becoming known for his flying machines by selling them when he could, giving flying lessons in them, and performing for crowds at weekends. He tried, without success, to interest the German army and navy in his planes. He made a meagre living but was mostly in debt and in grave danger. On one occasion a bracing wire parted when his aircraft was at 2,400 feet. He rode the disintegrating machine down into the trees and sur-

vived with only the slightest injuries, although his passenger died.

And so it went. Flying for promoters, taking great risks, and always cheating death.

When the war did come it came as a surprise to Fokker, as did a sudden turn in his fortunes. He was, he thought, just a businessman, and neutral about the conflict. He wanted only to make and sell his airplanes and was not concerned about who bought them. Virtually overnight every machine he had built was snapped up by the very same German army and navy that had coolly dismissed his earlier proposals.

Germany's military men, who now had an inkling of the combat potential of the airplane, called on Fokker to outdo the French in their efforts to make a plane serve as a flying gun platform. A Moraine-Saulnier monoplane was forced down behind the German lines in April 1915. The craft had a Lewis gun mounted in line with the propeller, and they noted the rather crude steel deflector plates on the propeller blades. To the Germans, this French idea was interesting, but they considered it a poor solution to the problem of firing a machine-gun through the arc of a propeller. They gave the problem to Fokker, who solved it in two days with a rod-and-cam device which interrupted the firing each time a propeller blade passed in front of the gun muzzle. The Germans were duly impressed, but remained indecisive, and it took three trial flights by the great ace Lieutnant Oswald Böelcke to convince the German Air Corps of Fokker's genius.

Orders poured in for Fokker's gun-synchonizing device and for his current monoplane which, when equipped with the device, proved devastating. It was more than a year before the first Allied fighter plane

Some of the kit of a well-dressed RAF pilot during the Battle of Britain.

appeared in action with a gun-interrupter gear. By his mid-twenties Antony Fokker had become a millionaire, but he still lived in a modest German boarding house with his dog and a pet monkey.

Throughout the war he continued to visit the front to consult the pilots who flew his planes. He got on well with them and relied on their advice and opinion in his efforts to design new and improved fighters.

Fokker's main problem in trying to compete with the latest Allied aircraft designs was inadequate power. The finest German aero engine of the day was the water-cooled 160 hp in-line Mercedes, but the entire factory output of the Mercedes engine was committed to the Albatros company. Fokker could obtain none for his own firm. This shortage inspired him to develop a better fighter that did not rely on increased power (speed), but rather on improved maneuverability and rate of climb. The Fokker Triplane featured three wings, a clean line, and very few wires and struts. Manfred von Richthofen, Germany's leading ace, was mightily impressed: "It climbs like a monkey and maneuvers like the devil." It was so maneuverable that most of his opponents never realized how slow it was, nor how limited its range. The Triplane had twin Spandau machine guns and an amazing rate of climb—ten minutes to 13,000 feet, a ceiling of nearly 20,000 feet, cantilevered wooden wings, cable-operated ailerons, balanced controls, and a landing speed of thirty mph. Its main fault was its seeming determination to ground-loop. Apart from that, it was strong and very difficult to shoot down.

However, the German army wanted speed more than any attribute offered by Fokker's Triplane and orders for the radical craft were

limited. Fokker still needed the Mercedes engine to develop the plane that he and the German army knew was required. In meetings with Richthofen's technical officer, Fokker proposed a contest among the leading aircraft makers to build a new plane, which the best German fighter pilots would evaluate. His condition was that each manufacturer should be able to use the Mercedes engine to power his entry. The trials were held in January 1918, and initially Fokker's design was a disaster. Von Richthofen flew it and clearly identified its severe problems. Undeterred, Fokker quickly corrected the problems, and Richthofen was amazed at the improvement. The German air corps implored Fokker to move immediately into mass production of his winning entry, which was in fact, a redesigned two-wing version of his Triplane. He was asked to name his price to build 400 machines. He asked for ten million marks and got it. He even had the satisfaction of watching Albatros and AEG, his primary competitors, ordered to build his design and to pay him a royalty on each such plane they produced. Thus was born the famous Fokker D-VII.

Nearly 1,000 D-VIIs had been built by the time of the Armistice, the first of them going to Baron von Richthofen's unit, JG-1. Richthofen was to die later in one of Fokker's Triplanes. Another World War I airman who flew the D-VII subsequently became famous in the next conflict: Reichsmarschall Hermann Goering of the German air force.

The first true fighter pilot was French Air Service Lieutenant Roland Garros who, on April 1, 1915, claimed the initial fighter victory of World War I. Garros was en route in his Moraine-Saulnier to drop two 155mm bombs

The British Sopwith Camel biplane fighter of World War I had twin synchronized machine guns and was highly maneuverable. Nearly 1,300 German aircraft fell to the pilots of these planes, which were also extremely good in the ground-attack role.

on a German railway station when he encountered an enemy two-seater aircraft. He got the Moraine into position and emptied three Hotchkiss gun strip magazines into the enemy plane, sending it down in flames.

On an early morning patrol in June 1917, the German fighter pilot Ernst Udet, at that point a raw twenty-one-year-old, spotted a French Spad VII biplane approaching him from the west. Udet was a relatively inexperienced flier with little flying time and few combat sorties flown, but he was already credited with having downed six enemy aircraft. When the two planes engaged, Udet was able to make out the word *Vieux* on the fuselage of his opponent's machine. It was common knowledge among airmen on the Western Front that the great French ace Capitaine Georges Guynemeyer flew a Spad with *Vieux Charles* painted on it, and Udet was now certain he knew the identity of the man he was fighting. Guynemeyer's score at that point was thirty kills. Udet quickly considered the odds against him. In addition to Guynemeyer's skill and fearsome reputation, his was a vastly superior aircraft to the Albatros that Udet was flying. The Spad was faster, climbed better, and was stronger and better able to take the stresses of aerial combat.

Udet tried every trick he knew, to no avail. His fate seemed sealed. Nothing worked until, finally, his luck improved for one brief moment and the Spad crossed through his sights. He tried to fire and found that both his guns were jammed. He beat furiously on the gun breeches, trying to free the jams without success. He saw that Guynemeyer was observing his predicament. Seconds passed and then, astonishingly, the

Frenchman waved and departed westward toward his own lines. Udet was confused. He knew, without any doubt, that Guynemeyer could have killed him easily in the few terrifying moments of their encounter, but had clearly elected to show mercy to his hapless, helpless enemy. There may be another explanation for the Frenchman's apparent act of chivalry in sparing the life of a still-combatant enemy pilot. Maybe Guynemeyer's guns were also jammed; maybe his ammunition was already expended, or perhaps he feared the German might, in desperation, decide to ram his plane. It seems probable, though, that Guynemeyer's act was that of a gentleman who hoped that he would be accorded a similar treatment if he were to one day find himself in Udet's situation.

Most historians agree that airmen in World War I behaved in a chivalrous manner. War correspondents remarked on the "knightly" behavior of the pilots on both sides. Willie Fry, a fighter pilot, wrote of the contrasting horror of the Battle of the Somme, and of Passchendale: "The public at home, and to a certain extent the ground troops in France, could not understand that, from the first, fighting in the air war was conducted on chivalrous lines and not with the hate largely generated by propaganda, justifiably in order to keep up the tempo of the war effort." This is not to argue that a chivalrous or gentlemanly approach to air fighting was dominant in the Great War; only that there is evidence that such acts and such behavior did occur then.

A World War II commander of JG-27, German air force, 1942–43, Eduard Neumann recalled: "It may be a little difficult for most people to understand today that the British

fliers always enjoyed our respect and sympathy. This is more conceivable if one knows that in all German pilots' messes in peacetime, the old veterans of World War I always spoke of the British pilots, of air combat with them, and of the British fairness in the most positive way."

In *Sagittarius Rising*, the remarkable memoir of his career as a fighter pilot in "the war to end wars," Cecil Lewis brought a wonderful clarity and color to his subject. Born in 1898, he joined the Royal Flying Corps, earning his wings at Gosport in February 1916 while still only seventeen years old. At eighteen, he was posted to France with No 56 Squadron, RFC: "The squadron was to be equipped with the SE5, the last word in fighting scouts, turned out by the Royal Aircraft Factory. It was fitted with a 140 hp Hispano Suiza engine and two guns: one Vickers synchronized and firing through the propeller by means of the new Constantinesco gear; and one Lewis gun, clamped onto the top plane and firing over the propeller. To change drums, the Lewis could be pulled down on a quadrant mounting, and in this position it could, if necessary, be fired straight upwards. The machine (for 1917) was quite fast. It would do about 120 on the level and climb ten thousand feet in twelve minutes. It could be looped and rolled and dived vertically without breaking up. Altogether it was a first-class fighting-scout (probably the most successful designed during the war), and was relied upon to re-establish the Allied air supremacy lost during the winter.

"I always regarded instruction as a come-down, a confession that the pilot was finished, no use at the front, and condemned to flip young aspirants round and round the aerodrome day after day on obsolete types of

top left: WWI ace Ernst Udet; above: Hermann Goering, future Luftwaffe chief; top right: The Nieuport of Canadian ace Billy Bishop, who was credited with seventy-two aerial victories; right: Wreck of a Bristol Fighter at Dayton, Ohio, in 1918.

OUT FOR VICTORY.

THE AIRMAN.
Who means to teach the Hun a lesson.

above: The badge of the Royal Flying Corps in
World War I.

machines. Of course, it was unreasonable, for competent instructors were most valuable to the rapidly expanding Force. Although their qualities were not necessarily those of successful active service pilots, they were equally important. A good instructor was, and still is, a pretty rare bird. It needs some guts to turn a machine over to a half-fledged pupil in the air and let him get into difficulties and find his way out of them. Instruction demands, besides, an ability to communicate oneself to another person (the secret of all good teaching), and not so simple as it sounds. Add to this great patience, the quality of inspiring confidence, and an extremely steady flying ability in the man himself, and it will be obvious that nobody need look down his nose at an instructor. All this I know now; then, the idea of flying an uninteresting machine condemned the thing out of hand, for flying itself, handling the latest and fastest types, trick flying, exhibitionism if you like, was all I cared about. Unconsciously quoting Shaw (with whom I was then unfamiliar), I thought, 'Those who can, do; those who can't, teach,' and prayed that I might not be posted to a Training squadron.

"The squadron sets out eleven strong on the evening patrol. Eleven chocolate-coloured, lean, noisy bullets, lifting, swaying, turning, rising into formation—two fours and a three—circling and climbing away steadily towards the lines. They are off to deal with Richthofen and his circus of Red Albatrosses.

"The May evening is heavy with threatening masses of cumulus cloud, majestic skyscapes, solid-looking as snow mountains, fraught with caves and valleys, rifts and ravines—strange and secret pathways in the chartless continents of the sky. Below, the land becomes an ordnance map, dim green and yellow and across it go the Lines, drawn anyhow, as a child might scrawl with a double pencil. The grim dividing Lines! From the air robbed of all significance.

"Steadily the body of scouts rises higher and higher, threading its way between the cloud precipices. Sometimes, below, the streets of a village, the corner of a wood, a few dark figures moving, glides into view like a slide into a lantern and then is hidden again.

"But the fighting pilot's eyes are not on the ground, but roving endlessly through the lower and higher reaches of the sky, peering anxiously through fur-goggles to spot those black slow-moving specks against land or cloud which mean full throttle, tense muscles, held breath, and the headlong plunge with screaming wires—a Hun in the sights, and the tracers flashing.

"A red light curls up from the leader's cockpit and falls away. Action! He alters direction slightly, and the patrol, shifting throttle and rudder, keep close like a pack of hounds on the scent. He has seen, and they see soon, six scouts three thousand feet below. Black crosses! It seems interminable till the eleven come within diving distance. The pilots nurse their engines, hard-minded and set, test their guns and watch their indicators. At last the leader sways sideways, as a signal that each should take his man, and suddenly drops.

"Machines fall scattering, the earth races up, the enemy patrol, startled, wheels and breaks. Each his man! The chocolate thunderbolts take sights, steady their screaming planes, and fire. A burst, fifty rounds—it is over. They have overshot, and the enemy, hit or missed, is lost for the moment. The pilot steadies his stampeding mount, pulls her out with a firm hand, twisting his head right and left, trying to follow his man, to sight another, to back up a friend in danger, to note another in flames.

"But the squadron plunging into action has not seen, far off, approaching from the east, the rescue flight of Red Albatrosses patrolling above the body of machines on which they had dived, to guard their tails and second them in the battle. These, seeing the maze of wheeling machines, plunge down to join them. The British scouts, engaging and disengaging like flies circling at midday in a summer room, soon find the newcomers upon them. Then, as if attracted by some mysterious power, as vultures will draw to a corpse in the desert, other bodies of machines swoop down from the peaks of the cloud mountains. More enemy scouts, and, by good fortune a flight of Naval Triplanes.

"But, nevertheless, the enemy, double in number, greater in power and fighting with skill and courage, gradually overpower the British, whose machines scatter, driven down beneath the scarlet German fighters.

"It would be impossible to describe the action of such a battle. A pilot, in the seconds between his own engagements, might see a Hun diving vertically, an SE5 on his tail, on the tail of the SE5 another Hun, and above him again another British scout. These four, plunging headlong at two hundred miles an hour, guns crackling, tracers streaming, suddenly break up. The lowest Hun plunges flaming to his death, if death has not taken him already. His victor seems to stagger, suddenly pulls out in a great leap, as a trout leaps on the end of a line, and then, turning over on his belly, swoops and spins in a dizzy falling spiral with the earth to end it. The third German zooms veering, and the last of that meteoric quartet follows bursting. But

For EVERY FIGHTER a WOMAN WORKER

UNITED WAR WORK CAMPAIGN

CARE for HER through The YWCA

Women factory workers in the First World War played a major part in the Allied victory, as they did in WWII. Temporarily replacing the men who had gone off to fight, they proved to their frequently skeptical male co-workers that they were every bit as capable and productive as the men they worked alongside.

Nieuport 28s of the Royal Flying Corps 95th
Pursuit Squadron in World War I.

such a glimpse, lasting perhaps ten seconds, is broken by the sharp rattle of another attack. Two machines approach head-on at breakneck speed, firing at each other, tracers whistling through each other's planes, each slipping sideways on his rudder to trick the other's gunfire. Who will hold longest? Two hundred yards, a hundred, fifty, and then, neither hit, with one accord they fling their machines sideways, bank and circle, each striving to bring his gun onto the other's tail, each glaring through goggle eyes, calculating, straining, wheeling, grim, bent only on death or dying.

"But, from above, this strange tormented circling is seen by another Hun. He drops. His gun speaks. The British machine, distracted by the sudden unseen enemy, pulls up, takes a burst through the engine, tank and body, and falls bottom uppermost and down through the clouds and

the deep unending desolation of the twilight sky.

"The game of noughts and crosses, starting at fifteen thousand feet above the clouds, drops in altitude engagement by engagement. Friends and foes are scattered. A last SE, pressed by two Huns, plunges and wheels, gun-jammed, like a snipe over marshes, darts lower, finds refuge in the ground mist, and disappears.

"Now lowering clouds darken the evening. Below, flashes of gunfire stab the veil of the gathering dusk. The fight is over! The battlefield shows no sign. In the pellucid sky, serene cloud mountains mass and move unceasingly. Here where guns rattled and death plucked the spirits of the valiant, this thing is now as if it had never been! The sky is busy with night, passive, superb, unheeding."

"Spin! I suppose nobody reading this today who is at all familiar with flying thinks anything of spinning. In 1916, to spin was a highly dangerous manoeuvre. A few experts did it. Rumour had it that once in a spin you could never get out again. Some machines would spin easier to the left than to the right; but a spin in either direction was liable to end fatally. The expression 'in a flat spin,' invented in those days, denoted that whoever was in it had reached the absolute limit of anger, nerves, fright, or whatever it might be. So spinning was the one thing the young pilot fought shy of, the one of two things he hoped he might never do—the other was, catch fire in the air. Now that I have done both, I assure you there is no comparison. Spinning is a mild stunt. It makes you a bit giddy if you go on long enough. It's a useful way of shamming dead when a Hun is on your tail; but fire in the air! That's a holy terror!"
—from *Sagittarius Rising* by Cecil Lewis

Instructors and students of the University of London Air Squadron getting ready for flight in their Avro Tudor biplanes.

"Ethics in war? The object of war is to kill and wound as many of the enemy as one can and to destroy all his supplies and communications in as short a time as possible. However, at the time I was there, it was an unwritten gentlemen's agreement between the fighter pilots of the Luftwaffe and the U.S. Army Air Force not to shoot an airman in a parachute."
—Lieutenant Colonel Robert M. Littlefield, USAF (Ret), formerly with the 55th Fighter Group, Eighth USAAF

"I never thought about ethics in regard to air combat. I had decided that even if the opportunity arose I would never shoot at a man in his parachute. Why I thought that way, I am not sure. It just didn't seem the right thing to do."
—Wing Commander Douglas "Duke" Warren, RCAF (Ret), formerly with Nos 66 and 165 Squadrons, RAF

"Fighting in the war does not know mercy. In case I don't kill the enemy, he will kill me. Fortunately, a fighter pilot never becomes a subject of bad conscience. He just defends his life, the lives of his comrades and the justice against cruel tyranny."
—Generalmajor Frantisek Fajtl, formerly with No 313 (Czech) Squadron, RAF

"Ethics went out the window. The principles of right or good behavior—the rules and standards of conduct certainly did not—could not apply to the combat fighter pilot's profession. This is where the beast came out, self-protection ruled—get that SOB before he gets you."
—Captain Jack Ilfrey, USAF (Ret), formerly with the 20th Fighter Group, Eighth USAAF

"If I saw them and could get to them,

I tried my very best to get 'em. That was why I was there."
—Colonel George L. Hollowell, USMC (Ret), formerly with VMF-224

"My own personal experience shows that there definitely was a spirit of 'camaraderie' of the knights of the air, at least in the European Theater. On 29th January 1945, I shot down Oberleutnant Waldemar Balasus in his Me 109G 'Blue 32.' After a ten-minute running battle, he was hit and bellied in at high speed on the snow-covered ground. He slid nearly a half mile, and when I passed over the wreckage at thirty feet the pilot was climbing out of the cockpit with one foot on the wing root and one foot still in the seat, and he rendered a snappy salute as I flew by. I was gone too quickly to return the salute but acknowledged it by rocking my wings. Incidentally, this pilot survived the war but died in 1989, just two years before I found out his name. Some German friends finally located his forty-nine-year-old son in 1996 and I received a picture of the man I shot down, from his son who works in a Hamburg bank."
—Major Walter Konantz, USAF (Ret), formerly with the 55th Fighter Group, Eighth USAAF

"Not much change in ethics from World War I. There was still fairness on both sides, as our great teachers from World War I would have never allowed any other way! Sad exceptions were happening on both sides, but the number was small!"
—Feldwebel Horst Petzschler, German Air Force, (Ret), formerly with X/JG51

Erich Hartmann, the German World War II ace of aces, recalled an incident when he was stationed in western France. A young German air

force leutnant had shot and killed a parachuting RAF pilot who had bailed out of his crippled Spitfire. When the German's squadron commander learned of the incident, he wanted to shoot the lieutenant, but others in the squadron convinced the commander to transfer the young man out of the squadron instead. There are many examples of airmen who were fired on while descending by parachute. Likewise, there are many instances on record of pilots who refused to take advantage of the opportunity to kill a foe coming down by parachute or in an otherwise defenseless position.

"By the rules of war it was justifiable to kill a pilot who could fight again. But few of us could bring ourselves to shoot a helpless man in cold blood."
—from Duel of Eagles by Group Captain Peter Townsend, formerly with Nos 43 and 85 Squadrons, RAF

"This is perhaps a convenient opportunity to say a word about the ethics of shooting at aircraft crews who have bailed out in parachutes. Germans descending over England are prospective prisoners-of-war and, as such, should be immune. On the other hand, British pilots descending over England are still potential combatants. Much indignation was caused by the fact that German pilots sometimes fired on our descending airmen (although in my opinion they were perfectly entitled to do so), but I am glad to say that in many cases they refrained."
—Air Chief Marshal Sir Hugh C. T. Dowding, Commander-in-Chief, RAF Fighter Command, during the Battle of Britain

"My habit of attacking Huns dangling from their parachutes led to many arguments in the mess. Some officers,

of the Eton and Sandhurst type, thought it was 'unsportsmanlike' to do it. Never having been to a public school, I was unhampered by such considerations of form. I just pointed out that there was a bloody war on, and that I intended to avenge my pals."
—Wing Commander James Ira "Taffy" Jones, formerly with No 74 Squadron, RFC and RAF

IN SEPTEMBER 1940, Squadron Leader John Kent, an RCAF officer, commanded No 303 (Polish) Squadron, RAF. On the 23rd, Kent downed a German fighter over the English Channel: "The 109 dived straight into the sea while he, apparently unhurt, drifted down in his parachute. I circled round him a couple of times and felt it might be kinder to shoot him as he had one hell of a long swim, but I could not bring myself to do it. Without waiting for him to hit the water, I turned for home. The Poles were fed up with me when I admitted that I could not bring myself to shoot the chap in the parachute and they reminded me of events earlier in the month when we were told that one or two pilots of No 1 Squadron had bailed out and had then been shot by German fighters. At the time the Poles asked me if it was true that this was happening. I had to tell them that, as far as I knew, it was, at which they asked: 'Oh, can we?' I explained that, distasteful as it was, the Germans were within their rights in shooting our pilots over this country and that, if one of us shot down a German aircraft over France and the pilot bailed out, then we were quite entitled to shoot him. But this was not so over England as, aside from anything else, he would be out of the war and might even be a very useful source of information for us. They thought about this for a bit and then said: 'Yes, we understand—but what

if he is over the Channel?', to which I jokingly replied: 'Well, you can't let the poor bugger drown, can you?' This remark was quite seriously thrown in my teeth when they heard about the 109 pilot I had just shot down. There was no doubt about it, the Poles were playing the game for keeps far more than we were."

Captain Richard E. Turner, Commanding Officer of the 356th Fighter Squadron, 354th Fighter Group, Eighth USAAF, described an incident in combat on 16 March 1944: ". . . I saw ahead of me the parachuting pilot of the 109 I had shot down a few minutes before. Pointing the plane at him, I flipped the gun switch to 'camera only' to get a picture, but the thought crossed my mind that the circuit had been known to foul up and fire the guns, so I restrained my desire to get a confirming picture of my victim. Instead, I turned aside, passing within thirty feet of him. I suppose when he saw me point straight at him, he fully expected to be gunned down, for he had drawn himself up and crossed his arms in front of his face as if to ward off the bullets, and when he saw me turn aside without firing, and waggling my wings as I passed, he started waving his arms and grinning like a Cheshire cat. I thought as I climbed that, since he had provided me with my tenth victory, he deserved a break. I just hoped he'd live to spread the word that Americans didn't shoot helpless pilots in parachutes. Maybe the Germans would follow suit."

Though a civilian, the celebrated aviator Charles Lindbergh spent part of the Second World War flying with U.S. Marine Corps and Navy fighter squadrons in the Pacific. On May 24, 1944, he was flying with three marine pilots off the coast of New Ireland on a reconnaissance and strafing mission: "Out to the coast line—four F4U Corsairs abreast, racing over the water—I am the closest one to land. The trees pass, a streak of green; the beach a band of yellow on my left. Is it a post a mile ahead in the water, or a man standing? It moves toward the shore. It is a man.

"All Japanese or unfriendly natives on New Ireland—everything is a target—no retrictions—shoot whatever you see. I line up my sight. A mile takes ten seconds at our speed. At 1,000 yards my .50 calibers are deadly. I know just where they strike. I cannot miss.

"Now he is out of the water, but he does not run. The beach is wide. He cannot make the cover of the trees. He is centered in my sight. My finger tightens on the trigger. A touch and he will crumple on the coral sand.

"But he disdains to run. Each step carries dignity and courage in its timing. He is not an ordinary man. The shot is too easy. His bearing, his stride, his dignity—there is something in them that has formed a bond between us. His life is worth more than the pressure of a trigger. I do not want to see him crumple on the beach. I release the trigger.

"I ease back on the stick. He reaches the tree line, merges with the streak of green on my left. I am glad I have not killed him. I would never have forgotten him writhing on the beach. I will always remember his figure striding over the sand, the fearless dignity of his steps. I had his life balanced on a muscle's twitch. I gave it back to him, and thank God that I did so. I shall never know who he was—Jap or native. But I realize that the life of this unknown stranger—probably an enemy—is worth a thousand times more to me than his death. I should

never quite have forgiven myself if I had shot him—naked, courageous, defenseless, yet so unmistakably a man."

Captain Eddie Rickenbacker, the American ace of the 94th Aero Squadron in World War I, made this diary entry on March 10, 1918: "Resolved today that hereafter I will never shoot at a Hun who is at a disadvantage, regardless of what he would do if he were in my position." Of that perspective he later wrote: "Just what influenced me to adopt that principle and even to enter it into my diary I have forgotten. That was very early in my fighting days and I had then had but few combats in the air. But with American fliers the war has always been more or less a sporting proposition and the desire for fair play prevents a sportsman from looking at the matter in any other light, even though it be a case of life or death. However that may be, I do not recall a single violation of this principle by any American aviator that I should care to call my friend."

By the beginning of World War II, the large numbers of aircraft and airmen involved, the airspeeds, the technical sophistication, and the armaments, had all changed dramatically from those of the Great War, and these changes inevitably influenced the conduct of all the participants.

"I shot an Me 109F down on 25 March 1945. The pilot bailed out from a vertical dive at about 7,000 feet. I felt quite elated that his parachute opened, and was quite contented with having destroyed the enemy aircraft. However, had my CO been on the mission, he would probably have had fits about me not attacking the pilot on the parachute. F. W. Lister, DSO,

far left: Captain Don Gentile of the U.S.A.A.F. 4th Fighter Group, with his crew chief at their Debden, England base in World War II; at top: German fighter pilots in a time out of war.

Goxhill control tower.

DFC and bar, had no time whatever for live Germans—or anyone else who might be enemy killers. Our work was air-to-ground—so we were killing German soldiers every day. Soldiers versus airmen? Not much difference to most of us."
—Flying Officer E. A. W. Smith, RAF (Ret), formerly with No 127 Squadron

Pilot Officer Richard Hillary of No 603 Squadron, RAF, fought in the Battle of Britain, was badly burned, and became one of Archibald McIndoe's plastic surgery "guinea pigs." Hillary's book, *The Last Enemy*, was one of the finest to come out of World War II. In it he recalled: "The voice of the controller came unhurried over the loud-speaker, telling us to take off, and in a few seconds we

were running for our machines.

"I climbed into the cockpit of my plane and felt an empty sensation of suspense in the pit of my stomach. For one second time seemed to stand still and I stared blankly in front of me. I knew that that morning I was to kill for the first time. That I might be killed or in any way injured did not occur to me. Later, when we were losing pilots regularly, I did consider it in an abstract way when on the ground; but once in the air, never. I knew it could not happen to me. I suppose every pilot knows that, knows it cannot happen to him; even when he is taking off for the last time, when he will not return, he knows that he cannot be killed.

"I wondered idly what he was like, this man I would kill. Was he young,

was he fat, would he die with the Führer's name on his lips, or would he die alone, in that last moment conscious of himself as a man? I would never know. Then I was being strapped in, my mind automatically checking the controls, and we were off."

RAF Pilot Officer Roger Hall, No 152 Squadron, flew Spitfires in the Battle of Britain. In his book, *Clouds of Fear,* he remembered: "I watched the Hurricane turn over on its back and fall away. The pilot himself was on fire and he fell away from the machine. As the Hurricane went into a shallow dive, he released his parachute, but as it opened, its shrouds caught fire. The pilot, who had now succeeded in extinguishing the flames on himself, was desperately trying to

climb up the shroud lines before they burnt through. I witnessed this scene with an hypnotic sort of detachment, not feeling myself able to leave it as I circled above. I was thankful to see the flames go out and the parachute behave in a normal manner. I felt a great surge of relief well up inside me, but it was to prove short-lived.

"Two 109s appeared below me coming from the north, and travelling very fast towards the south as though they were intent upon getting home safely to France.

"I disregarded the pilot hanging from the parachute and diverted my attention to the 109s, which appeared to be climbing slowly. I felt I should get my first confirmed aircraft now and turned on my back to dive on them. When I was in the dive I had my sights well in front of the forward 109 with lots of deflection, for I was coming down upon them vertically. The leading 109 was firing and I looked to see what he was firing at but could see no other aircraft near him. Then I saw it all in a fraction of a second, but a fraction that seemed an eternity.

"He was firing at the pilot at the end of the parachute and he couldn't possibly miss.

"I saw the tracers and the cannon shells pierce the centre of his body, which folded before the impact like a jack-knife closing, like a blade of grass which bends toward the blade of the advancing scythe. I was too far away to interfere and now was too late to be of any assistance. If to see red is usually a metaphorical expression, it became a reality to me at that moment, for the red I could see was that of the pilot's blood as it gushed from all the quarters of his body.

"I expected to see the lower part of his body fall away to reveal the entrails dangling in midair but by some miracle his body held together. His hands, but a second before clinging to the safety of the shroud lines, were now relaxed and hung limp at his sides. His whole body was limp also, like a man just hanged, the head resting across one shoulder, bloody, scarlet with blood, the hot rich blood of youth which had traversed and coursed through his veins for perhaps not more than nineteen or twenty years. It had now completely covered and dyed red an English face which looked down on but no longer saw its native soil."

The cockpit of an F-4 Phantom fighter.

Richard Hillary: "My first emotion was one of satisfaction, satisfaction at a job adequately done, at the final logical conclusion of months of specialized training. And then I had a feeling of the essential rightness of it all. He was dead and I was alive; it could so easily have been the other way round; and that would somehow have been right too. I realized in that moment just how lucky a fighter pilot is. He has none of the peronalized emotions of the soldier, handed a rifle and bayonet and told to charge. He does not even have to share the dangerous emotions of the bomber pilot who night after night must experience that childhood longing for smashing things. The fighter pilot's emotions are those of the duellist—cool, precise, impersonal. He is privilged to kill well. For if one must either kill or be killed, as now one must, it should, I feel, be done with dignity. Death should be given the setting it deserves; it should never be a pettiness; and for the fighter pilot it never can be."

"A good fighter pilot must have one outstanding trait—aggressiveness. Without that he's of no use to his squadron or the Air Force."
—Major John T. Godfrey, USAF (Ret), formerly with the 4th Fighter Group, Eighth USAAF

"We were told that some Americans had been shot as they descended by parachute, but I have no personal knowledge of that happening. We were also told that if our planes were damaged in combat to the point that we had to abandon them, we would not be fired on if we dropped our landing gear. Again, I have no personal knowledge as to whether this was true or not."
—2nd Lieutenant Robert N. Jensen, USAF (Ret), formerly with the 55th Fighter Group, Eighth USAAF

Richard Hillary: "In a fighter plane, I believe, we have found a way to return to war as it ought to be, war which is individual combat between two people, in which one either kills or is killed. It's exciting, it's individual, and it's disinterested. I shan't be sitting behind a long-range gun working out how to kill people sixty miles away. I shan't get maimed: either I shall get killed or I shall get a few pleasant putty medals and enjoy being stared at in a night club."

"There is no working middle course in wartime."
—Winston Churchill

"Nothing is ever done in this world until men are prepared to kill one another if it is not done."
—from Man and Superman by George Bernard Shaw

"The RAF seemed to have a different social feeling from the other services. Those who cared about such things noted a preponderance of 'minor public school' men; they called them the Brylcreem Boys in semi-affectionate recognition of the fact that no 'gentleman' would use such cheap hair cream. None of this mattered. What was significant was the character of a man who wanted to fly fighter planes. He needed to be competitive and scornful, eager for a chance to prove himself; he needed also a rarer combination of qualities: he had both to be young and alert, yet attach no great importance to his life. This was the requirement that came before patriotism, political belief or even skill in flying. It was not like being in the infantry where, even during the slaughters of the Western Front in 1914–18, you had a better than even chance of surviving. If you flew more than a certain number of missions in 1940—you were not likely to come back. This did not mean that all the pilots were reckless, willing to risk their lives for the sake of the chase and kill above the clouds; nor did it mean that they had to be more patriotically motivated. It meant only that they had to have, at heart, some indifference to dying. The public were encouraged by Churchill's speeches to believe this indifference was heroic; the pilots themselves did not see it as such. Far from subscribing to the myth, they tried to subvert it. They cultivated understatement in a private slang; they came close to callousness: they claimed to feel nothing."
—from The Fatal Englishman by Sebastian Faulks

Battle, n. A method of untying with the teeth a political knot that would not yield to the tongue.
—from The Devil's Dictionary by Ambrose Bierce

From a conversation with General Adolf Galland, formerly with the German air force in World War II: "In summer and autumn of 1940 I shot down twenty-one Spitfires, three Blenheims and one Hurricane. The battle was tough but it never violated the unwritten laws of chivalry. We knew that our conflict with the enemy was a life and death struggle. We stuck with the rules of a fair fight, foremost being to spare the life of a defenseless opponent. The German Air Sea Rescue people therefore picked up any RAF or American pilot they found floating in the Channel, as well as the German airman.

"To shoot at a pilot parachuting would have seemed to us an act of unspeakable barbarism. I remember the circumstances when Goering mentioned this subject during the

Battle of Britain. Only Mölders was present when this conversation took place near the Reichsmarshall's train in France. Experience had proved, he told us, that especially with technically highly developed arms such as tanks and fighter aircraft, the men who controlled these machines were more important than the machines themselves. The aircraft which we shot down could easily be replaced by the English, but not the pilots. As in our own case it was very difficult, particularly as the war drew on. Successful fighter pilots who could survive this war would be valuable not only because of their experience and

knowledge but also because of their rarity. Goering wanted to know if we had ever thought about this. 'Jawohl, Herr Reichsmarshall!' He looked me straight in the eyes and said, 'What would you think of an order directing you to shoot down pilots who were bailing out?' 'I should regard it as murder, Herr Reichsmarshall,' I told him, 'and I should do everything in my power to disobey such an order.' 'That is just the reply I had expected from you, Galland.' In World War I similar thoughts had cropped up, but were just as strongly rejected by the fighter pilots."

"I always associated the German pilot

in his aircraft as just 'the aircraft trying to shoot me down.' However, the beast in me was always there, making every effort to stay alive. I can remember saying to myself 'Ha ha, you SOB, I gotcha.' The after feelings were various—remorse, guilt, elation, joy . . . victorious. I think my worst experience along this line was the day my flight of four P-38s got jumped in North Africa. I saw my wingman firing at one, while two enemy aircraft were coming in on him. It was like they were right in front of my eyes, but out of my range. I did my damnedest to get over to help him, but saw him hit the silk, and I suddenly had to fight for my life. I got

left: A Hawker Typhoon pilot responds to a "scramble" order; above: USAF armorers prepare to attach a missile to an aircraft during the Gulf War in the 1990s.

two Fws, but lost the other three in my flight. A most awful feeling of help-lessness. There was a bond between us that most people can never attain in a lifetime . . . somewhat akin to love of your fellow man, I guess. Then there were the feelings in reverse, when my flight leader literally saved my life when I was badly shot up. I find all this hard to explain."
—Captain Jack Ilfrey, USAF (Ret), formerly with the 20th Fighter Group, Eighth USAAF

"This time I had the feeling I had killed a man, but there was no time for remorse. If it were he this time, it could be me the next. In the mount-ing frenzy of battle, our hearts beat faster and our efforts became more frantic. But within, fatigue was deaden-ing feeling, numbing the spirit. Both life and death had lost their importance. Desire sharpened to a single savage purpose—to grab the enemy and claw him down from the sky."
—Group Captain Peter Townsend, RAF, formerly with Nos 43 and 85 Squadrons

Five-foot six-inch Zdzislaw Krasnodebski of No 303 (Polish) Squadron, RAF, learned to fly as on of the first pupils of the new Polish Flying School in 1925. On September 6, 1940, 303's Hurricanes lifted from London's Northolt airfield under orders to attack a formation of German bombers that was approach-ing the capital.

On intercepting the enemy bomb-ers, Squadron Leader Krasnodebski maneuvered to open fire on one of them and was himself hit at that moment. The glass covering the instruments of his cockpit panel shat-tered and the fuel tank immediately in front of it poured aviation spirit into the cockpit. The fuel instantly ignited, forcing Krasnodebski to abandon the airplane as quickly as he could. Pulling

far left: RAF Hurricane pilot Bob Doe; top left: 357th FG pilot George G. George; top right: Jim Browning also flew with the 357th at Leiston in WWII; below: Brendan "Paddy" Finucane of No 65 Squadron, RAF, was credited with twenty-eight aerial victories.

far left: Squadron Leader Brian Lane was a Spitfire ace and Battle of Britain pilot; opposite right: High-achieving Adolf Galland was a top German fighter leader.

the hood back, he rapidly undid the harness and seat belt, disconnected the radio lead and the oxygen mask, and jumped from the burning Hurricane.

Wishing to avoid becoming a slowly descending, defenseless target for the Me 109s in the area, he delayed opening his parachute until he thought it reasonably safe to do so. At that point he could not find the parachute handle and wasted precious seconds searching for it as the earth seemed to rush up to meet him. He finally located the handle, deployed the parachute, and found that he was floating down in complete silence. He then became aware of the tremendous pain in his badly burned hands and legs. Fortunately for him, the speed of his brief fall, caused by the delay in opening his parachute, extinguished the flames of his clothing and helped to preserve the integrity of the parachute and the shroud lines.

As he descended toward a landing in a farm field, several members of the local Home Guard emerged from the bushes and moved toward the spot where the Pole was likely to land. They raised their rifles and Krasnodebski thought his time had come.

It was his yellow Mae West life jacket that saved him. The British home defense troops recognized it, if not the unfamiliar Polish uniform, and refrained from shooting him. He landed yelling "Polish officer, Polish officer" to the Home Guard men. They took him straight to a hospital for burn treatment.

Flight Lieutenant Findlay Boyd of No 602 Squadron, RAF, was thought to be one of the best pilots in his squadron. His no-nonsense approach to his work as a fighter pilot in the Battle of Britain, and, in particular, his attitude

PER·ARDUA·AD·ASTRA

McM

WAR SAVINGS CAMPAIGN 1943
PRESENTED BY THE AIR MINISTRY
IN RECOGNITION OF
SUCCESSFUL ACHIEVEMENT IN
WINGS FOR VICTORY WEEK

top right: Former 4FG pilot Jack Raphael; center: Eighth Air Force poker chips; right: Former 56FG leader Hub Zemke; top right USAF F-15 Eagle pilots head for their planes in the Gulf War.

to air fighting, earned him considerable respect from many but left others perplexed. For Boyd, shooting down an enemy pilot produced exhilaration, and if the foe bailed out, Boyd would try to shoot him as he dangled in his parachute. If the enemy pilot safely reached the sea, he would try to shoot him there. Boyd saw it as the only logical option. He believed that no German airman should be allowed to get back to his base to take off again and shoot at more RAF airmen.

"Some of your questions about fighter pilots have a bearing on the people I

Hurricane pilots of No 303 (Polish) Squadron based at RAF Northolt, London, in October 1940. Their commander was Canadian Johnny Kent., second from left.

have met in my civilian life, and in general, I liked the fighter pilots I met a lot better than many of the civilians."
—Colonel Walker M. Mahurin, formerly with the 56th Fighter Group, Eighth USAAF

It was the evening of August 15, 1940 and the pilots of No 54 Squadron, RAF, sprawled in near exhaustion on the grass of RAF Manston in Kent. Colin Gray said: "I've had enough today. I reckon the Huns have too. I'm just dying for a beer, a good meal and bed." Al Deere shared his fellow New Zealander's wants, but just then they were ordered up and the pilots of Deere's flight ran for their Spitfires. The nine Merlins roared into life and in seconds were lifting from Manston's

grass surface. The controller called: "Hello, Hornet Leader, seventy plus, Angels twenty heading Dungeness—Dover. You are to engage fighters."

Squadron Leader James Leathart of No 54 Squadron took his pilots up to 25,000 feet and they bounced the Me 109s. Al Deere concentrated on a Messerschmitt that he was chasing southward in a gentle dive towards France. Suddenly it was Deere being chased by two 109s and in an instant the instrument panel in his Spitfire exploded, the engine screamed as it was hit and his windscreen was quickly filmed with black oil. The 109s turned for France and the New Zealander for England. The crippled Spitfire floated across the Kentish cliffs and Deere managed about 1,500 feet

of altitude as he got ready to leave the doomed plane.

He jettisoned the canopy and rolled the plane onto its back to drop out. On the way, his parachute pack caught on something as the Spitfire began to dive upside down. He freed himself and his parachute opened in time to save him but it also deposited him within 100 yards of where his plane, *Kiwi II*, had impacted and exploded.

He lay there collecting his parachute and his thoughts, when two airmen arrived introducing themselves as ambulance personnel on their way to Kenley. "We thought we might help." "Excellent service," thought Deere.

In a few hours he was in treatment at the East Grinstead Cottage Hospital

Bob Stanford-Tuck had twenty-nine aerial victories to his credit in WWII. After the war Tuck was a mushroom grower in Kent; right: A still from the 1968 film *Battle of Britain*.

burn unit, where the pioneering plastic surgery techniques of Archie McIndoe were being perfected. McIndoe's famed "guinea pigs," the horrendously burned and battered Battle of Britain pilots whose wounds he treated, would forever be grateful for the many healing miracles he achieved. Al Deere's injuries were relatively minor, and in the night he checked himself out of East Grinstead and caught a train back to base.

"In the Navy's Pre-Flight School, one half of the time was devoted to body-contact athletics. Football was rough enough. We also played basketball with ten men on a side, and the referee was there for the sole purpose of breaking up fist fights. We played water polo at the deep end of the pool, and the instructor cracked the knuckles of anyone caught hanging on to the side. Push ball was another form of mayhem that was designed to inflict bodily harm on the other guy. In hand-to-hand combat we learned how to knife-fight, break a man's neck, go for the jugular, break an arm, dislocate a shoulder, apply a knee to the groin, and so on.

"Physical fitness training where competition was stretched one step further to combativeness was re-emphasized at each phase of the flight training program, which lasted about ten months at that time [1942].

"I think it's fair to say that we came out of the cadet program with a certain killer instinct and an aggressive approach to survival. When it came time for me to go into combat with the Japanese, the issue was uncomplicated. They were out to kill me and I was determined to do unto them before they did unto me."
—Commander William E. Copeland, USN (Ret), formerly with VF-19
"The obscure future date on which

I should at last go into action had always been remote in my mind, imperfectly realized, even, I suspect, deliberately shut out. Now, suddenly, with a brief order, it had become startlingly clear and close at hand. For months after, with a few brief moments of respite, I was to live hypnotized not so much by the dread of death—for death, like the sun, is a thing you cannot look at steadily for long—as by the menace of the unforeseen. Friends, mess companions, would go out on patrol and never come back.

"As the months went by it seemed only a matter of time until your turn came. You sat down to dinner faced by the empty chairs of men you had laughed and joked with at lunch. They were gone. The next day new men would laugh and joke from those chairs. Some might be lucky and stick it for a bit, some chairs would be empty again very soon. And so it would go on. And always, miraculously, you were still there. Until tomorrow . . . In an atmosphere you grew fatalistic, and as time went by and left you unscathed, like a batsman who has played himself in, you begin to take liberties with the bowling. You took unnecessary risks, you volunteered for dangerous jobs, you provoked enemy aircraft to attack you. You were invulnerable: nothing could touch you. Then, when one of the old hands, as seemingly invulnerable as yourself, went West, you suddenly got cold feet. It wasn't possible to be sure—even of yourself. At that stage it required utmost courage to go on—a sort of plodding fatalism, a determination, a cold-blooded effort of will. And always alone!"
—from *Sagittarius Rising* by Cecil Lewis

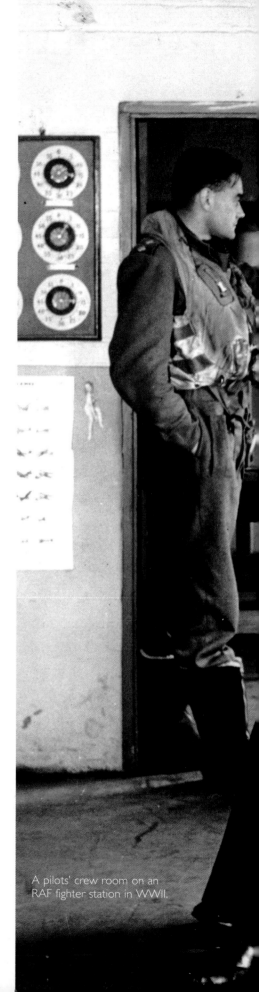

A pilots' crew room on an RAF fighter station in WWII.

An F-4 Phantom of the German air force at Schleswig, northern Germany.

A NATURAL?

Major Urban Drew shot down two German jet fighters while flying a P-51 Mustang with the 361st Fighter Group in World War II.

"I believe I had natural flying ability in that I took to flying easily and had no trouble going through pilot training. I believe those flyers who had this natural flying ability had the edge on those who did not, those who got shot down more than they should have. The fighter pilots in my squadron, for the most part, had it; there were only a few who did not and normally they did not last very long."
—Colonel Bert McDowell, Jr., USAF (Ret), formerly with the 55th Fighter Group, Eighth USAAF

"Natural-born flyers . . . birds only!"
—Captain William O'Brien, USAF (Ret), formerly with the 357th Fighter Group, Eighth USAAF

Captain Alan Leahy, RN (Ret), flew the Hawker Sea Fury with No 801 Squadron in HMS *Glory* during the Korean War: "Natural pilots found it easier to achieve high scores in air-to-air and air-to-ground exercises as they were less likely to fly with skid, slip or excessive negative or positive G forces on the aircraft. If the aircraft is not in balanced flight, the weapon will not go where the sight is pointing."

"Many fighter pilots were not natural-born flyers. Werner Mölders had some problems at the beginning of his [flying] career. Hans-Joachim Marseilles, on the other hand, was to my knowledge, a natural-born flyer."
—Generalleutnant a.D. Günther Rall, German Luftwaffe, (Ret)

As one who flew Mirages and F-16s in the Israeli Air Force, Colonel Gidi Livni, IAF (Ret), believes that flying ability is not the most important feature of the successful fighter pilot: "I knew some pilots who lacked this gift of nature, yet scored more than ten kills. Often, agility, aggressiveness and a 'hunting sense' are more important than the ability to fly the aircraft smoothly with co-ordination.

Flight Lieutenant Charles M. Lawson, RAF (Ret): "Every [RAF] fighter pilot [in the Second World War] had about two hundred hours of flying logged before joining a squadron. That was gained through Elementary Flying Training, where you first learned to fly; Service Flying, where you gained experience in all aspects such as instrument flying, night flying, advanced aerobatics, formation flying and navigation, where you finally earned your wings. After that you spent time in an Advanced Flying Unit, which helped you prepare for combat duty, and finally, you were posted to an Operational Training Unit where you first flew Spitfires and were trained in actual aerial warfare and low-flying techniques. Of course, every trainee didn't get that far, as you could be 'washed out' at any time if your performance was unsatisfactory or if your instructor believed that you were not cut out to be a pilot.

"To be a fighter pilot you had to be trained on single-engine aircraft such as a Harvard, be of a certain size and age, desire to fly fighters, and be recommended for the role by your Service Training Flying Instructor.

"Did we have natural flying ability? I didn't think so! World War II required so many pilots that all of them couldn't be naturals, but I do think that the intensive training helped immensely in sorting out the boys who could handle the task. Some were instinctively better than others and became the leaders on the squadrons, but I never knew anybody on our squadron who lacked ability or guts."

"I don't recall any pilots I would consider to be naturally born with pilot ability. Once a pilot got to the point where both he and the aircraft were 'one,' he would have the ability to become a superior pilot because he didn't have to think about driving his aircraft and, instead, could think about missions, victories, escort, weather and all the other requisite things. One doesn't get to be a champion acrobatic pilot unless he practices hour after hour at his trade. One has to have the desire to excel and the energy to spend the time and effort to do so, before he achieves success. I knew some pilots during the wars [WWII and Korea] that I thought were really good in training, but that was mostly because they wanted to be. Another factor was that one had to be good if he wanted to survive."
—Colonel Walker M. Mahurin, USAF (Ret), formerly with the 56th Fighter Group, Eighth USAAF

"The general consensus was, if we could get four or five missions under our belts, we'd be in pretty good shape. We had pretty good instructors. They worked for the German Air Force."
—Captain William O'Brien, USAF (Ret), formerly with the 357th Fighter Group, Eighth USAAF

"Natural flying ability was very important. I started flying lessons at age fifteen, owned my own airplane at age eighteen, and had a private pilot's license and 250 hours of flying time before I entered the aviation cadet program. I knew many fighter pilots with better-than-average ability, and most did well in combat. This is not to say that the best went to fighters and the worst to bombers and transports, although there is some truth to this assumption. Some misfits occasionally slipped into the fighter

The North American Harvard / T-6 / SNJ was the advanced flying trainer for most RAF, USAAF, and US Navy pilots of WWII.

groups. The sole purpose of some of these 'fighter pilots' was to survive the war, not necessarily to win it. I knew one pilot in my squadron who finished his tour of 270 combat hours, about sixty-five missions, and openly bragged that he had never fired his guns."
—Major Walter Konantz, USAF (Ret), formerly with the 55th Fighter Group, Eighth USAAF

"I became a 'natural-born flyer' through instinct. Both of my parents were somewhat adventurous. My father was a World War I fighter pilot and instructor. After the war he joined the Texas National Guard. My first ride in an airplane, as a very young kid, was strapped on my mother's lap in a Jenny while my father flew it. He also

did some motorcycle, speedboat, and auto racing, while I tagged along, reveling in the thrill of it all. I did some of the same as a teenager. Even though some of us were considered to be natural-born flyers, we still had to learn to be masters of our aircraft."
—Captain Jack Ilfrey, USAF (Ret), formerly with the 20th Fighter Group, Eighth USAAF

1ST LIEUTENANT Henry C. Woodrum, USAF (Ret), formerly with the 344th Bomb Group, Ninth USAAF: "As the pilot of a Martin B-26 Marauder bomber, I never saw a good dogfight. When enemy fighters got through our fighter cover, they flashed past the formation so fast that we saw only fleeting glimpses of them. Our tail-gunners

saw a few skirmishes, but no sustained engagements. When I finally did see one, it was from the ground.

"While flying my thirty-fifth mission, to attack bridges across the Seine River near Paris on May 28, 1944, I was shot down by German flak. The following day I contacted members of the Resistance. They took good care of me and for five days I was hidden in a small tavern where I ate well and was treated royally as the guest of a fine couple, Carlos and Maria. They spoke excellent English, having spent many years in New York City where Carlos had led a rhumba band at the Waldorf-Astoria. They were glad to aid an American.

"On June 2nd, I was moved to an apartment on the top floor of a building on the rue de Chantier in Versailles. There I was the guest of Charles and Delise. From their windows I could see the Eiffel Tower in the distance to the northeast. Less than four miles to the east I could see German aircraft taking off from Villacoublay aerodrome. At first there was only moderate activity, but on D-Day things really picked up, reaching a peak which was sustained for several days.

"Flights began arriving at dawn to refuel and fly shuttle runs to the invasion beachhead throughout the day. Often they returned individually, badly battered and damaged. Just before dark, they would refuel and fly to the more remote fields of eastern France to escape the night-bombing RAF. I was always amazed to witness their massed departures because they were so unorthodox compared with American techniques.

"Their takeoff procedure seemed to consist solely of a left climbing turn after gear-up. There was no regular interval between takeoffs. Each plane departed when it was ready, started the left climbing turn, and merged with the swirl of snarling aircraft.

"The first big mission departure I saw was on D-Day, before I learned of the Normandy landing a hundred miles or so to the west. It was about seven o'clock in the morning, and when I heard the sound of so many aircraft engines I pulled a chair over to the window and waited for something to happen. The revving of the engines continued, then suddenly a red-nosed Me 109 with red wingtips leapt up in a very steep angle, starting a left climbing turn. Others followed immediately, and with each new launch the stack grew higher and higher, forming one great ever-enlarging corkscrew-shaped spiral. When the last plane was airborne there must have been at least

fifty fighters involved, and the whole shebang just seemed to collapse as the leader nosed his plane down, accelerating as the others tagged along in a sort of indiscriminate mass, behind, alongside, underneath, and above him. Without an apparent pattern, they looked like a swarm of bees—either there was no precision or the utmost precision possible. I couldn't tell which was the case, but they never flew it any other way. I watched them many times and never saw them have any trouble, but I couldn't figure out how they could keep everyone in sight.

"That morning they headed westwards and I wondered why such a large flight was in the area. It was far and away the largest I had seen, for most of the previous flights had been only small patrols.

"About two hours later I heard several aircraft coming in from the west and I looked out the living room window. The red-nosed Messerschmitt slanted hurriedly in, knifing down for a landing. There was a sense of urgency about it because he made no attempt to set up a preliminary pattern but maintained airspeed all the way through a long, straight in approach. Before he touched down, out of sight behind the trees ringing the field, others flew in from the same direction. Several trailed smoke, one badly. Then another group came in, milling about over the field as they set up a landing priority. Some were Focke Wulf Fw 190s. There must have been nearly 100 fighters all together. I remember counting more than sixty, and I missed several flights.

"Throughout the next half hour they continued to straggle in, revving their engines, jazzing them like kids in hot rods. The jazzing bit made me cringe. In B-26s we wanted power all the way in.

"A neighbor on a nearby balcony excitedly called Delise over and told her about the invasion. Delise came running inside, calling me by the name on my forged identity card which said I was a forty-two-year-old merchant from Deurdan.

"'Albert, Albert. Le debarquement. Le debarquement est ici.' She was so excited I couldn't get much information from her. We turned on the radio, but the German-controlled French station had nothing so I switched to the Yankee Doodle network. They were playing music—Glenn Miller.

"After a pause and the phrase of the song which identified the station, the announcer gave the latest report on the invasion, with a detailed analysis of the whole story. Then I knew where the Jerries had been and why their numbers had increased after takeoff. The Luftwaffe was probably being diverted from all over Europe to Normandy. It was tremendous news, and to me it was a real boost. I kept listening to the radio all day and telling Delise what was happening. The French radio stations told us nothing, but all morning cryptic messages were transmitted over both AFRS and the BBC. The BBC's were delightful. 'Pierre, there is a red, red rose in the icebox for you.' 'Marcel, your interest will be due in the 12th.'

"I often tuned in to the BBC after that to catch those messages and to get the news at dictation speed, which gave me a chance to take notes.

"Later, one of our own teams went into action. Charles learned that the marshalling yard was full of German tanks which were supposed to depart for Normandy last night. I wrote a note to an English agent who had contacted me, and he got the message off by portable radio units at about eight o'clock in the evening. Just before midnight it got results, for the RAF started a raid which lasted until one a.m. The marshalling yard was closer to our apartment than I had thought, and for the entire raid there were flashes from exploding bombs, crumbling buildings, the thudding wham of antiaircraft batteries and the almost constant rocking of our building on its foundation. We finally went to bed at about three a.m.

"The next morning I was still sleepy and stayed in bed dozing until something awakened me. It was an unfamiliar sound, a sort of popping. Then came sounds I recognized— racing aircraft engines. I jumped out of bed and ran over to the window, dragging the sheet with me. Coming straight toward me at not more than fifty feet above the roof was an American P-51 Mustang going flat out. Close behind it were five Fw 190s, sort of bunched together, flying like bees again, and all of them were taking pot shots with their 20mm cannon at the poor old Yankee boy.

"I saw all this simultaneously, before the planes flashed by just over the rooftop. They were coming from the airfield towards the apartment, headed northwest. I could even see the pilot, tensely hunched over the controls. He was wearing helmet and goggles and his chute straps showed plainly against the darker color of his A2 jacket; a patch of white scarf was visible at his throat. The checkered yellow, or maybe checkered yellow and white nose of the plane was clear and distinct. The aircraft was unpainted bright aluminum, and its marking—black letters and the national insignia—stood out. It had a bubble canopy, the first one I had seen.

"As they passed overhead, I whirled and ran through the apartment, across the living room to the window on the other side of the building. The fighters actually dipped lower going away, for our building

stood on the side of a slope, and the terrain fell away toward the center of Versailles. They were soon out of sight, and I was sure the Mustang jockey was a goner. I turned away from the window and for the first time realized Delise was standing by my side and that I was wearing only a pair of shorts.

"She looked at me and said, 'Albert, l'Americain?'

"'I think so, Delise, yes.'

"'Ah . . . pas bon.'

"I went back into the bedroom and put on my pants and uppers. Then, suddenly, Delise opened the door, shouting.

"'Albert, ici, ici!'

"I followed her quickly into the living room and onto the tiny balcony. A couple of minutes had passed, with the battle unexpectedly continuing, but the tide had changed. Coming toward us from the southwest, still at rooftop level, were the six fighters, but leading the pack was a lonesome Fw 190, frantically trying to escape the P-51 pilot who was relentlessly hosing him with .50 caliber slugs in short, accurate bursts. Behind were the other four Jerries, holding their fire for fear of hitting the first Fw. Not more than 300 yards separated the first plane from the last.

"I began to really sweat out the American, though, because the Jerry was playing it cozy by heading straight for an antiaircraft battery in a patch of woods. Sure enough, it opened fire. The Fw waggled his wing and the ground fire stopped, but the P-51 did the same thing and they didn't shoot at him either. Its pilot continued firing, and the law of averages caught up with the German plane. It exploded in a great, angry, red and black and orange burst.

"The Mustang pilot flew through the debris, but he was again being shot at, so he banked toward Villacoublay a mile or so away. As he

left: New Zealanders Colin Gray and Al Deere were among the highest-achieving RAF Spitfire pilots of the Second World War; below: An RAF fighter pilot runs for his warming Spitfire during the Battle of Britain.

10¢

SKY FIGHTERS

SPRING ISSUE

A THRILLING PUBLICATION

BUY WAR BONDS AND STAMPS FOR VICTORY!

BLACK NEST OF CALAIS
An Exciting Action Novel
By STEUART M. EMERY

A FLIER GOES TO SEA
A Smashing Novelet
By SAM MERWIN, JR.

started a low pass over the field, all the ack-ack in the base opened up, even on their own planes. The three on the left, nearest Paris, turned left to avoid the flak, but the other one was too far to the right and had to turn to the right to stay clear. The Mustang turned also, heading for the lone Fw which apparently lost sight of him momentarily. Within thirty seconds the Yank was sitting on his tail, taking pot shots at the Luftwaffe again. The two planes were now heading toward me, almost on the same track they had flown on their first pass over the house earlier. The other three were completing a wider turn and were grouped some distance behind, and even though no physical change had occurred, they didn't seem to have the pouncing snarl or the look of the hunter so apparent in their first low-level pass. They straggled, trying to catch up, but they were too far back to save their buddy.

"Again, I raced through the apartment to the other window. As the two planes came over, the thunder of their engines was punctuated by the short, ammo-saving bursts of the .50 calibers. Scraping over the rooftops, twisting and yawing, they crossed the city, and finally the Fw 190 began to trail smoke. It nosed down into the horizon to merge with the red flame and black smoke-cloud of impact just west of town. We learned later that the pilot got out alive but was badly injured.

"The Yank racked the 51 around in a steep chandelle, right off the deck. Two of the other190s flashed past and pulled up also, but the third was a little further back and turned north, away from the tiger who continued his turn, diving a little now. With the height advantage for the first time, the Yank began firing on a dead pigeon. Smoke immediately trailed

from the Fw, but the 51 pilot had to turn away as the other two planes closed in on him. The distressed Fw 190 limped away, trying to get back to Villacoublay, but crashed north of town several miles from the base. Now only two Germans were left, and the American had put a little distance between their planes and his.

"By this time I was absolutely going nuts. It was all I could do to keep from shouting in English. Everybody else was excited too. People had come out on the rooftops of nearby apartments, and the balconies were full of men and women silently cheering for the crazy, lone American. I knew he would have a rough time from here on out. The last two wouldn't give him any breaks. On the other hand, they were wary, which might be in his favor. They flew out of sight on the deck southwest of the city. It was quiet for a minute or two

War correspondent Virginia Irwin of the *St. Louis Post-Dispatch* interviewing Ralph "Kid" Hofer at Debden, England, home of the 4FG in WWII.

and the rooftop audience became restless, frustrated.

"Then they returned, still on the deck, and the Yank was miraculously in the middle. They made a long pass across town while the Mustang closed to a range from which he couldn't miss—I figured he was very low on ammunition. The 190 was trying to outrun him this time, but when he saw his nemesis so close behind, the pilot pulled up frantically. The .50s cut loose in a brief, shattering blast. The 190 nosed straight up and its engine died. As the prop windmilled almost to a stop, the plane began to stall about 1,000 to 1,500 feet off the deck, and the pilot bailed out, opening his parachute immediately. At first its slow, billowing trail made me think it would never open, but it blossomed full and white only a few feet above the trees between me and the Eiffel Tower, standing very tiny in the distance.

"Now the odds were even up, and what had seemed an eternity to me had really happened in just a few minutes. I began to worry about other German fighters getting airborne to aid their shot-up air patrol, but they were either engaged elsewhere or were unable to fuel up, fearing attack from other aircraft.

"In the distance I could see the last two planes in another long, low arc. The American had started a gradual swing to the west, but he was not about to leave the deck. The Jerry was still behind him, but his guns were silent now, indicating he might also be low on ammunition. When they disappeared over the rim of the rolling hills west of the city the Mustang was taking evasive action, and I was sure the dogfight was almost over. The Jerry had the advantage and was sure to hold it. A moment later, a black, blotchy mush-room of smoke billowed upwards.

"I knew then that one hell of a good pilot had bought the farm. He had given it everything he had and reduced the odds from five to one to even before the end, and I wondered what he had thought when only that one Fw remained. Just a few pilots had ever shot down five German aircraft in one day.

"I noted the time and tried to fix the approximate location of the action and also made a mental note of the aircraft markings, determined to confirm the four victories if I ever got back to England. I just couldn't forget the way the man had flown, dreaming up tactics as he went along, playing it by ear, only to have his luck run out a little too soon.

"The spectators on the rooftops felt as I did. They stood up slowly, stretched, gestured with their hands and went back inside. They seemed to feel a personal loss, almost as if they had been with the pilot themselves, pushing him on to victory with their will alone. They had prayed for his survival, now they prayed for his soul.

"Delise said nothing but went into the kitchen and returned with two glasses and a bottle of Armagnac. She filled the glasses, raised hers and said, 'Le pilote Americain.' Her voice was soft and her eyes brimmed. I nodded and we drank. I had a couple more—alone.

"I sat there thinking about the pilot and the action-packed few minutes just passed. Suddenly, after three weeks of almost no war at all, it was back with me again and then suddenly gone. All I could do was sit there and think.

"Twenty minutes later, Charles, Delise's husband, came home. He was very excited and laughed as he asked if we'd seen the fight. 'Did you see the American kill those Germans?' 'Yes', I said. 'We saw. He got four of them. Four out of five.'

"He looked at me and grinned, taking another sip of brandy, and suddenly I wanted to hit him, he looked so smug.

"'Non. No, no. He got five. He got them all. I see . . . everything. Especially the last. It was magnificent.' He said this in a mixture of French and English, the way we always conversed. He launched into a stream of French I couldn't understand, but it didn't make any difference because I could tell that he was certain the Yank had gotten all five. We had several more brandies before Charles calmed down enough to explain what had happened.

"'Charles, how do you know he got them all?'

"'Because, I saw. Especially the second, third, and fifth, you know. The last was near me. I was at the garden. I have to rake—to hoe, you see. The last one he did not even shoot much. They came near, so fast. There is this little hill, with woods. The planes almost skim the ground. The American goes zip, like so, around the hill once, and the German follows, but in a greater circle. It is like the cat and mouse. The second time the American plane slows—and abruptly—its wheels drop out, you know? The German goes in, towards the American, now so much slower, and they are almost sideways, but he loses control of his machine. Only a kilometer or so from where I was standing he crashes in the woods. I jump up and down and wave my hoe and everybody does the same, but then the Germans come and we hide our smiles and I come home fast.'

"I thought about what must have happened. The American pilot was out of ammunition and had dropped his flaps and gear—everything—chopped his throttle, to slow down, forcing the German to turn in, risking a stall to make the German stall. The German didn't have much choice. If he didn't make one last try he would have wound up in front of the Mustang anyway—so he had to make the try.

"Everybody I saw for the next few days talked about the dogfight. Coming so soon after D-Day, it gave all of us, me especially, a tremendous boost in morale.

"The plans to get me out of France by a night pickup from a wheat field didn't materialize, and it was early September before I reached London. I reported the dogfight during my debriefing, but by that time I had forgotten a key factor—the aircraft marking, including the squadron code.

"Years later, I spent several days in the Air Force Historical section at Maxwell Field, Alabama, trying to learn the name of the pilot by reading all operational reports submitted by Mustang pilots for the period. Now, I do not even remember the exact date. I narrowed it down to twenty-one pilots. Several were killed on the missions involved and others had been killed later in Germany. One noted: 'confused fighting at house-top level in the Paris area,' but claimed no victories.

"As of now, the identity of the American pilot has never been verified, and it's too bad. But there's one thing I know. Even if I never find out who he was—it was the best damned dogfight I'll ever see!"

Two of Japan's greatest fighter pilots of World War II were Lieutenants Hiroyoshi Nishizawa and Toshio Ohta. Nothing mattered more to them than their function as fighter pilots. Their skills, their determination, and their intensity made them extraordinarily dangerous to the Allied flyers who faced them in combat. Unfazed when they found themselves on the wrong

Mark Hanna at the controls of Spitfire MH434 at Duxford, England.

end of the odds, or in an engagement with aircraft of superior performance to that of their Zeroes, they prevailed repeatedly.

Physically, Nishizawa was the antithesis of the image of a fighter pilot. He weighed only 140 pounds, was pale and gaunt, and looked extremely malnourished, with his ribs showing prominently through his skin. He was chronically ill with skin diseases and suffered from malaria.

Quiet and reserved, he impressed most of his fellow pilots as being cold and unfriendly, a loner who would often go an entire day without saying a word to anyone. But no Japanese fighter pilot commanded and deserved the admiration and respect of his peers more than Nishizawa. Few, if any of them, were more dedicated and committed to the fight than he, and none was to match his score. Referred to as "the Devil" by those who flew with him in combat, Nishizawa came into his own when the fight was on. The famous Japanese World War II ace, Lieutenant Saburo Sakai, recalled how Nishizawa "seemed to become one with his plane; how the seeming genius of his gentle touch at the controls made his fighter respond almost magically, in ways Sakai had never seen before. His aerobatics were at once brilliant and totally unpredictable. He flew like a bird—better than a bird."

Friendly, amiable, and gregarious, Toshio Ohta was an exact opposite to Nishizawa in personality, but no less intense in the air. He enjoyed a good joke, was quick to join in with his friends in a good time, and even quicker to come to the aid of a fellow pilot who needed help in the air or on the ground.

Like Nishizawa, his superb flying skills and his brilliance in combat brought Ohta considerable

recognition in their Wing at Lae, New Guinea, and throughout the Japanese air forces. Ohta's final score was thirty-four.

"Men, welcome to the 4th Fighter Group. You have been assigned here after completing your training in the 3rd Air Force. There you were required to comply with a myriad of rules, regulations, and orders, governing your conduct in the air and on the ground. The requirements were designed to promote safety for you and your fellow flyers during your training period. Now you are trained combat fighter pilots assigned to a top fighter group in the Eighth Air Force. We have the same rules, but we are capable and aggressive, and you must be also. To this end, whenever you leave the base on a flight, do not return to land until you have broken those rules. BUT DON'T GET CAUGHT, or you will never fly with this group again! Secondly, if anyone 'Prangs a Kite' while stunting, he's out!"
—Colonel Don Blakeslee, formerly Group Commander, 4th Fighter Group, Eighth USAAF

Having achieved fifty-one victories as a fighter pilot with the 50th Sentai in the Philippines and Burma theatres of World War II, Sergeant Satoshi Anabuki was the top living Japanese fighter ace in the 1990s. He twice downed three enemy aircraft in one day, and, on October 8, 1943, claimed three B-24s and two P-38s in a single combat. His final victory of the war came in June 1945 when he brought down a B-29 Superfortress. He had good eyesight but admitted to being "clumsy and not good at piloting." However, he refused to quit, worked harder than his fellow pilots, and was quite successful as a fighter pilot. Like

so many high-achieving fighter pilots, Anabuki credited his success to shooting from close range.

In World War I, he was known by his men as der Rittmeister. Today he is the stuff of legend, one of the first fighter pilots and certainly among the greatest of all time, the man everyone knows as "the Red Baron," Manfred Freiherr von Richthofen.

That eighty Allied aircraft fell to his guns is certainly remarkable. Of interest too is the judgement made during his pilot training in 1915, that he was "lacking in natural aptitude."

In time, Richthofen met Oswald Böelcke, the father of the German fighter arm, and eventually became his protégé. Richthofen's career took off in the summer of 1916 when Böelcke selected him for the new Jagdstaffel 2, and he joined their first offensive patrol in mid-September. Flying an Albatros DII, he downed an FE2b over Cambrai that day, and that night he celebrated by ordering a silver trophy cup from Berlin to commemorate the kill. It was the first of many such cups.

On October 28, the great Böelcke, having been credited with forty aerial victories, was killed in a midair collision. Manfred von Richthofen succeeded him as Germany's leading ace, averaging one kill a week.

On November 23, 1916, Richthofen shot down the top Royal Flying Corps ace of the time, Major Lanoe George Hawker, the "English Böelcke." His victories mounted quickly and on January 16, 1917, he was awarded the Order Pour le Mérite, colloquially known as the Blue Max, and was given his first command,

left to right: 357th FG pilots Major Richard Peterson, Major Leonard Carson, Captain John England, and Captain Clarence Anderson. All flew Mustangs from their Leiston base.

that of Jasta 11. In December 1916 Richthofen had begun to paint parts of his plane a bright scarlet to show the other side whom they were up against when they encountered him. He felt that the red paint might intimidate some of his opponents, and he was right. His score continued to build, to sixty by September 1917, to seventy in March 1918, to eighty by April 20, 1918. On the 21st, however, his luck ran out.

Flying from their airfield at Bertrangles, the Sopwith Camels of No 209 Squadron, RFC, led by Captain Roy Brown, engaged Richthofen's fighters over the Somme Valley. The German's red Triplane came through Brown's sights and the Canadian's twin Vickers guns brought a quick finish to the spectacular life and career of the Red Baron.

"I can't remember the time when airplanes were not part of my life and can't remember ever wanting anything so much as to fly one. Once I had started, I had to keep flying.

"But it was not until I was seventeen that I finally got into an airplane. At that time I felt I had come to the place where I belonged in the world. The air to me was what being on the ground was to other people. When I felt nervous it pulled me together. Things could get too much for me on the ground, but never got that way in the air. Flying came into my mind like fresh air into smoked-up lungs and was food in my hungry mouth and strength in my weak arms. I felt that way the first time I got into an airplane. I wasn't nervous when I first soloed. There was excitement in me, but it was the nice kind you get when you are going home after a long, long happy time away."
—Major Don S. Gentile, formerly with the 4th Fighter Group, Eighth USAAF

below: A first day cover dedicated to 20FG ace Captain Jack Ilfrey; right: South African fighter ace of the Battle of Britain, Squadron Leader Albert G. Lewis, who flew with Nos 85 and 149 Squadrons, RAF.

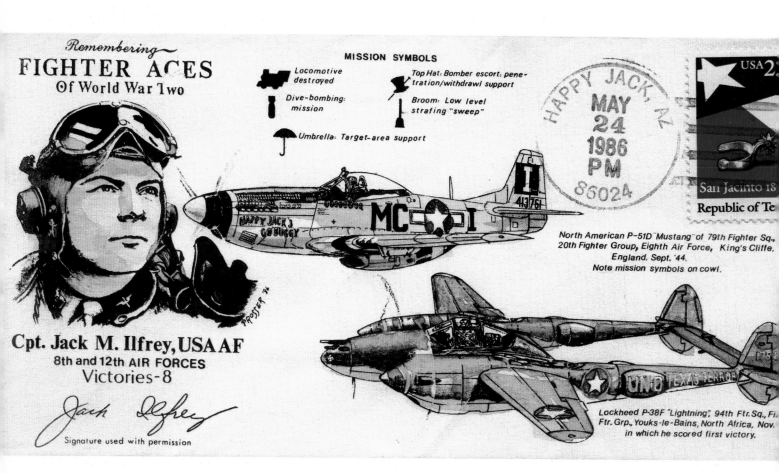

A still from *The First of the Few*, depicting the story of Spitfire designer R. J. Mitchell.

ON SCREEN

In his autobiography, American World War I ace Captain Eddie Rickenbacker wrote that after the war, the Universal Studios producer Carl Laemmle made frantic efforts to sign Rickenbacker to perform in a motion picture about his wartime adventures. Laemmle offered the ace a reported $100,000., and Irving Thalberg, Laemmle's assistant, badgered Rickenbacker throughout a cross-country train journey, trying to wear down the airman's resistance to signing. When Rickenbacker had finally had enough, he threatened to sue Laemmle for personal harassment. Rickenbacker: "I could just see myself up there on the screen making movie love to some heroine. I was fully aware of my potential influence upon the youth of America, and I intended to continue to do my best to inspire them by both deeds and words. Depicting myself in the movies, I felt, would degrade both my own stature and the uniform I so proudly wore."

Ever since the First World War, most of the movie industry's films on military aviation themes have tended to stray wildly from reality. Even today, when studio committees consider the potential merits of an aerial epic, reality often seems to receive a lower priority than, say, the projected profit from the sale of toys and other by-products related to the picture. Authenticity frequently gets short shrift with arguments such as "We'll do it all with effects; it'll be cheaper and no one will know the difference"—as nonexistent fighter planes flash across the screen at impossibly high speeds in equally incredible maneuvers. The screenplay calls for the hero to be a womanizer—never mind that the real guy was and is happily married. That won't play in Peoria. Action in the air, action on the ground. That's the ticket.

It was and still is routine for the

producers to hire a "technical advisor" to provide a layer of credibility for their film. But in general, they seem disinclined to listen to the guy whose name and credentials they proudly list in the film credits, much less take his advice.

One glaring example was the 1942 Universal production *Eagle Squadron*, produced by Walter Wanger. It was the first major American movie on the air war, made after the Japanese attack on Pearl Harbor in December 1941 and America's entry into the war. Unfortunately, the movie trivializes the activities of the first three American fighter squadrons in the European war. Several members of the Eagle Squadrons—the American volunteer pilots serving with the RAF—and many prominent English guests were invited to the London premiere in July 1942. USAF Colonel Lee Gover, a former RAF Eagle and USAAF 4th Fighter Group pilot, recalled: "The film was so far-fetched from actual air combat . . . it was really embarrassing." Most of the American pilots in the theater that evening wanted to walk out en masse, but felt that, as invited guests, it would be impolite. Still, some of them could stomach no more of the film after the first half hour, and quietly departed by a side door. Bill Geiger, another Eagle, remembered: "That movie upset everybody, and Squadron Leader Chesley Peterson in particular. We had been told that it would be a documentary, like the March of Time of those days. We all felt that we had been double-crossed. Pete was so bitter about it that he never responded to any requests for information for publicity about the Eagles from that day forward."

After the release of *Eagle Squadron*, even the popular correspondent Quentin Reynolds, who

had been well-liked and highly regarded by the Eagles—whom he frequently entertained in his London flat, and who had delivered the opening narration in the film—was therafter refused access to Peterson's airfield. Gover: "We were just another RAF squadron trying to do our best. We deserved, and wanted, no special attention., because of our American background, which overshadowed the British and Commonwealth squadrons who were doing the same job and with whom we had to fly."

Major General Carroll W. McColpin, USAF (Ret): "When they had the showing at the premiere in London, they made a big deal about it, getting a lot of Eagles, as many as they could at the time, in to see it, and I don't know of anybody that stayed through the picture. I'd say the bulk of us got up after the first thirty minutes, and walked out. The English were madder than hell at us . . . the protocol people, because there was supposed to be a lot of public relations and, anyway, you didn't walk out on the King, for God's sake. So, it was just a farce. Typical Hollywood. It was insulting at the time because here were the people being bombed all the time, and fighting the damned war, and then they come in with a thing that's obviously so phoney even a little kid would know it."

Generally, television has not shown itself to be much more earnest than the movies in pursuit of authenticity where stories of fighter pilots are concerned. The 1988 UK production *Piece of Cake*, based on Derek Robinson's 1983 novel of the same title, is a case in point. Many Royal Air Force fighter pilots who were operational on squadrons in Britain in the early years of the Second World War

have stated that they were appalled by the representations made in the TV production. They saw little similarity between the real pilots they knew, and were themselves at that time, and those portrayed in the multi-part epic.

It is also the case that no Spitfires were operating in France in the period before the Battle of Britain, contrary to the way *Piece of Cake* represented events. On the plus side, the aerial sequences were flown and filmed with wonderful graphic power and the fighter planes were worked hard and well by consumate professionals.

So-called "creative license" comes into play, even in big-budget productions, and limitations or directorial whims tend to dictate a fudge here or a larger compromise there. Actual events and people often become unrecognizably distorted. Those who lived the events reshaped on film, and all who care about accurate representation of history, can only wince.

War movies, and especially air war movies, have, for the most part, not found great favor with film critics over the years. Once America had entered the Second World War and Hollywood had a full year of war movie making under its belt, *New York Times* film critic Bosley Crowther summed up the product to date: "By and large, the general quality of motion pictures this past year has reflected the confusion and uncertainty which the war has exposed in Hollywood. Producers have plunged willy-nilly into purely escapist pictures or have made the war out to seem illusory by dodging it into old routines." Film historian Clyde Jeavons has suggested that it was not the nature of these early films so much to inform the public, as "to stimulate . . . to wrap the war up in attractive packaging

THOSE GUYS IN THE SKIES WITH WINGS ON THEIR HEARTS BRING A ROARING NEW THRILL TO YOURS!

WARNER BROS. PRESENT

There's new glory in the air and this is the story that tells of it – with the flyin'-est, fun-lovin'-est Yankee Doodle daredevils the adventure-screen has yet seen!

FIGHTER SQUADRON

The Flying Fist of the Air Force!

IN COLOR BY TECHNICOLOR

If it had wings they'd fly in it! If it had skirts they'd fight for it!

STARRING
EDMOND O'BRIEN · ROBERT STACK · JOHN RODNEY

DIRECTED BY
RAOUL WALSH

PRODUCED BY
SETON I. MILLER

with TOM D'ANDREA · HENRY HULL written by SETON I. MILLER Additional Dialogue by Martin Rackin Music by Max Steiner

the most famous of the Battle of Britain pilots, commented on the 1968 Guy Hamilton-Harry Saltzman production of *Battle of Britain* filmed mainly in Spain and at Duxford in Cambridgeshire: "I think they did it quite well, but the air battle was fought in the air, and nothing was going on on the ground. They had to try and make something there into a film. For example, we never got off the airfield during the actual battle. There were no girlfriends or pubs or things. We just didn't get off the airfield. How could we? We were so short of pilots! So, the filmmakers, in order to make a story, had to have a girlfriend, driving up and meeting her pilot at a pub. Well, there was none of that at all. There was before and there was after, but not whilst the battle was on. There was no relief whatsoever. Oh, we were moved as a squadron up north for a week, but that was only in order to refurbish and get some new pilots in and give them a quick bit of training, and then back again to Hornchurch. We were 'on readiness' or we were so bloody tired we were just dead. There was no glamour about it, really. That seems trite, but there wasn't any at the time. We didn't feel much glamour, I can tell you."

"The fighter pilot was a very individual person, often not shown correctly on TV or in the press. Hollywood often gave the wrong picture and so did the UFA in Potsdam on our side. Too much propaganda, not enough truth."
—Feldwebel Horst Petzschler, German air force (Ret, formerly with X/JG51)

Early in 1943, Colonel Robert L. Scott had a hit on his hands. Scott, one of the highest-scoring American fighter aces, had gained prominence as commander of General Claire Chennault's

and sell it to the people." In his fine book on aviation films, *Celluloid Wings,* James H. Farmer wrote: "Within such a context, death for the Allies, if not the enemy, was often antiseptic and painless. The protagonists were naively heroic and unashamedly patriotic. Such story lines were usually entertaining and professionally smooth but generally were far removed from the harsher reality." Crowther did feel that "the one encouraging trend has been the growing one towards actuality films

[documentaries], indicated mainly in the short product and more recently in the films of the OWI [Office of War Information]. Still very much on the periphery of screen entertainment, these films at least are foretelling a more thoughtful and realistic fashion in screen fare. This is the brightest prospect for films in the months—or years—ahead."

Group Captain Alan C. Deere, No 54 Squadron, RAF (Ret), among

Nicholas Pennell, Edward Fox, and Ian McShane in a scene from *Battle of Britain*.

23rd Fighter Group, descendants of the Flying Tigers, in China. At the age of thirty-four, he was back in the States, dictating his virtually guaranteed best-seller, *God Is My Copilot*, to stenographers at Scribner's, the New York publishing house. So hot was this still-unpublished book that Scott was offered and accepted the then-staggering sum of $100,000 for the screen rights by Warner Brothers. Before accepting the Warners' offer, Scott cleared the movie deal with

General Henry H. "Hap" Arnold in Washington, who told him: "You make it authentic and you make it faithful to the Air Force and you make them pay you." Clearly, Arnold believed strongly in the value of showing the American public what the Army Air Forces were doing around the world. His agenda included the ultimate creation of a separate and independent United States Air Force, and he knew the importance of effectively promoting his service.

In Hollywood, the Warners assigned Hal Wallis to produce the movie version of Scott's book, and he brought in the writer Steve Fisher to do the screenplay, working with Scott. Fisher wrote the first draft and met Scott. "When Steve showed it to me it began to take on all these things . . . malaria [which Scott never contracted], and a Japanese pilot called Tokyo Joe, which had nothing to do with the book." James Farmer stated in *Celluloid Wings*: "Scott, a happily-married man of many years, most strongly objected to the script's equally fictitious love affair." "I loved my wife I never wanted anything like that in the movie!" and after his many protests the China-based love interest was deleted.

After several months' delay, *God Is My Copilot* finally began filming in August 1944. When it was released early in 1945, the moviegoing public seemed to like the film; the critics did not. Bosley Crowther: "Obviously Warner Brothers took the title of Colonel Robert L. Scott's war book . . . much more literally than the author did. For their rip-roaring film . . . is heavily and often embarrassingly larded with piety. For Colonel Scott's popular, vivid story of his career in the Far East has been turned by the Warners into another, rather cheaply theatrical war film." James Farmer: "Sadly much of the Peter Milne dialogue degenerates into 1942 vintage pulp fiction that pleased neither Scott nor critics—'Okay you Yankee Doodle Dandies, come and get us. I'm going to drop one of you right in Chennault's lap. Where are you gangsters? Come up and get a load of that scrap metal you sold us.' "

Scott recalled his feelings about the film: "Chennault had evidently sent a letter to Arnold and had used the phrase, 'I am being made to look over-sympathetic in the role projected by Raymond Massey.' So I got orders to report to the Pentagon to view the film with all the staff. And, man, I had to sit there and see that corny film in which so little is true. They made me have that malaria attack which never did happen . . . and here I sat in the Pentagon with every general and most of the admirals watching *Copilot*, embarrassed as hell. When it was over they applauded. Arnold stood up

and said, 'I see no oversimplification or over-sympathetic performance. I think it's a good picture.' I wanted to say, 'General, what are you talking about? It never did happen like that!' And with 'Big Mike' sitting back in that P-43 saying, 'Fear can sabotage the strongest heart . . .' well, it's amazing how they make a movie!"

Yet another aspect of air war entertainment was the multi-episode serial, produced for both film and radio in the war years. In these brief potboilers, all pretence of reality went out the window; pulp-fiction adventure and fantasy were all. Such efforts as *Flight Lieutenant, Captain Midnight, Sky Raiders, Smilin' Jack, Hop Harrigan,* and *Adventures of the Flying Cadets* were avidly followed by teenage and pre-teen would-be fighter pilots who, years later, remembered being inspired by these serials. They counted them among the influences which led them to follow their dream and become real fighter pilots.

In 1948, Warner Brothers returned to the fray with *Fighter Squadron,* directed by Roaul Walsh and starring Robert Stack and Edmund O'Brien. With a script that had "orders from above" prohibiting the USAAF P-47 pilots jettisoning their long-range drop tanks in combat, credibility took a beating from the word go. Colonel Lee Gover was assigned to the *Fighter Squadron* project and he recalled the drop tank matter: "During the war they asked us to bring the belly tanks home if we could, because they were scarce at first. But when we got into a dogfight we didn't give a damn who said don't drop 'em. We dropped them."

Actor Jack Larson played the part of Shorty, the youngest pilot in the squadron. Of the director, Larson recalled: "Raoul Walsh was a very

imposing personality, tough with that tough voice of his. He wore boots and riding pants and had that eye patch [he had lost an eye filming an early western]. He never really rehearsed you. He was interested in timing and dialogue and didn't deal with the actors much. He never gave you any direction except to say, 'Pick it up, kid, the scene's on its ass', or 'I could

drive a truck through that pause.' Of *Fighter Squadron,* James Farmer wrote: "Leaving Hollywood for the last time in July, Gover, who appears as an extra in the film's pub sequences, returned home with mixed emotions. Although satisfied with the flying scenes that he led in the air, Gover remained dissatisfied with much of the script. The sense of frustration would grow

as veteran pilots, friends who had flown for the film and knew and felt what it had really been like in the war, were killed. For many of these men, it was their last chance to see the story told before giving their lives during the Korean conflict. Commenting on the film, Gover admitted: 'I knew the movie wasn't very good, just too much Hollywood nonsense in the damn

thing. I told them at the time, but no one would listen.' "

"I think most of the good fighter pilots I have known were pretty much 'devil-may-care' types, especially during wartime. I'm sure it was partially to avoid becoming too obsessed with the inherent dangers of being a pilot in combat. Although they were not

Robert Shaw as a character modeled on "Sailor" Malan, in the 1968 film production *Battle of Britain.*

very intellectual, they were extremely intelligent and, in most cases, team players. Of course, the successful ones were exceptionally competent aviators and knew their aircraft's capabilities as well as its limitations. They all really enjoyed flying and particularly aerobatics."
—Lieutenant Commander H.B. Moranville, USN (Ret)

"I think that *Top Gun* came out before I actually joined the Air Force. It was out when I was applying to join the University Air Squadron, and I think it was the big, glamorous 'look what

I can do, this is great, and we're all wonderful heroes, and everything is happening at twice the speed' . . . I wouldn't say the job is mundane. It's not at all, but the movie is exaggerated. Some of the sequences are great to watch, but they're not realistic as far as what happens day to day on the squadron. The actual stuff that goes with it, all the big talk and everything, I don't know. The Americans themselves might find some of it a little more akin to what they do, but as far as the RAF . . . we operate on a completely different level to what *Top Gun* is showing you. It's something that

people watch and they know all the lines to, and it's good fun to throw them around every now and again. It's good fun to watch. I don't think there is anybody on the squadron who hasn't seen it, or anybody who would object and say, 'Oh, I'm not watching it. It's rubbish.' It's more of a laugh. Pilots like watching aeroplanes flying on screen and it always looks brilliant when you see it with the cameras, but I don't think the way they interact with each other is anything quite like what goes on on the squadron."
—Flight Lieutenant Helen Gardiner, No 43 Squadron, RAF

below: Former RAF Group Captain Peter Townsend during the filming of *Battle of Britain* in 1968; opposite: Aces Douglas Bader, left, and James "Ginger" Lacy on set during the filming of *Battle of Britain* in 1968.

THE IRON

The North American P-51D Mustang long-range escort fighter is certainly among the best military aircraft in history.

IN THE LATE 1930s, the British Air Ministry believed that, with the Vickers-Supermarine Spitfire and the new Hawker Hurricane, both Rolls-Royce Merlin-powered fighters, they could meet RAF Fighter Command's requirement for the defense of Great Britain. They had no particular interest in any other fighter types and certainly none in anything then being produced in the United States. There was simply no match for the speed, maneuverability, and fire power of the Spitfire at that time. The Spitfire was, however, rather short on range, and as the European war entered its fifth month it became clear to some in the British defense establishment that the RAF needed a fighter of greater range to meet the Italians' very real threat in Egypt and that of the Japanese to Singapore. The Air Ministry then decided that it required a thousand new fighters for delivery in 1941, and placed an order with Brewster in the U.S. for the Buffalo. But the American company could supply no more than 170 Buffalos during 1941, and the Air Ministry had to look elsewhere.

By the end of 1939, France too needed new fighters and agreed with the Curtiss Company of New York to purchase 420 Hawk H75A and 259 H81A fighters, an export version of the U.S. Army Air Corps P-40. The French were hoping that by 1941 the U.S. Army would let them buy P-38s and P-39s.

A joint Anglo-French Purchasing Commission (AFPC) was formed and after many complex and frustrating twists and turns featuring such players as Bell Aircraft, Lockheed, and Republic, in addition to Curtiss, the commission finally decided to order 667 export models of the Lockheed Model 322, a P-38 variant. It could not, however, be delivered in quantity until late 1941.

In June 1940, after France had fallen to the Germans, the RAF inherited the Curtiss aircraft ordered by the French, and came to regret th AFPC's commitment to the Lockheed 322. Furthermore, in late May Curtiss had changed its production planes, and was now offering the P-40D. Both the Army Air Corps and the RAF believed that this was a better plane than anything else available, and, what is more, it had an earlier delivery date. The RAF bought 471 of one version and 560 of a second, naming them the Tomahawk and the Kittyhawk.

However, the British still had a fighter requirement. The RAF needed more fighters than Curtiss alone could build and, even before the Curtiss Kittyhawk production program had begun, went shopping for another source of P-40 production. On February 25, 1940, they approached North American Aviation in Los Angeles, whose Harvard I

trainer had served them impressively since 1938, and asked the company's president, J. H. "Dutch" Kindelberger, to consider building P-40s for them.

Kindelberger's chief designer, a forty-year-old German engineer named Edgar Schmued, who had emigrated first to Brazil and then to the United States in 1930, had worked for North American since 1936. His fellow designers regarded him as quiet, friendly, and methodical—and as a man with a burning ambition to design and build the best fighter plane in the world.

He had been working on design ideas for several months, using a German engineering handbook called *Huette*, together with his own small notebook of technical formulae. Rumors that the British wanted North American to build P-40s for them had been circulating in the Los Angeles (Inglewood) factory, and Schmued was well prepared when Dutch

A Hawker Hurricane fighter being serviced at Exeter; right: A Messerschmitt Bf109 having force-landed on the French coast during the Battle of Britain.

Kindelberger dropped by his office one early March afternoon. He asked, "Ed, do we want to build P-40s here?" Schmued responded: "Well, Dutch, don't let us build a obsolete airplane. Let's build a new one. We can design and build a better one." Kindelberger: "I'm going to England in about two weeks, Ed, and I need an inboard profile, a three-view drawing, performance estimate, a weight estimate, specifications and some detail drawings on the gun installations to take along. Then I would like to sell that new model airplane that you develop." He told the designer to make it the fastest plane he could, and to build it around a man that was five feet ten inches tall and weighed 140 pounds. He said that it should have two 20mm cannons in each wing and should meet all design requirements of the U.S. Army Air Corps. With that, North American Specification NAA SC-1050 was issued. Work on the new fighter began on March 15, 1940.

Armed with the papers he had requested, Kindelberger left for Britain later that month, as Ed Schmued and his design team started to build a paper and plaster-of-Paris mock-up of the new plane. On Thursday, April 11, Sir Henry Self, director of the AFPC, signed a letter of intent to purchase 400 Model NA-50B fighters, and the greatest fighter of the war had been launched.

Lend-Lease had not yet started and Britain wanted to keep its costs down on the new plane, which was to be powered by an Allison engine. The agreed unit price of $40,000 was not to be exceeded by the manufacturer, who also undertook to deliver 320 aircraft between January and the end of September 1941, and fifty per month thereafter. It was estimated that the actual cost to Britain would be $37,590 per plane.

By merging his earlier fighter design concepts and a laminar-flow airfoil, Schmued shaped the Model NA-73. The RAF contracted with North American for 320 of the new model in late May 1940, although final official British approval was not given until July 20, after the fall of France and the start of the Battle of Britain.

The design assignment was apportioned to several specialized groups under Schmued's supervision. He estimated that a hundred days would be needed to build the first experimental airplane. The British required North American to have the airplane flight-tested, debugged, and in production within one year. There were many concerns within the company about the new wing and how it might perform. Exhaustive testing proved its viability, and brilliant scheduling and co-ordination resulted in that first airplane being completed in both engineering and the shop in 102 days—almost exactly as promised. In 1984, Schmued reflected: "We could never build another plane today in a hundred days as we did then. Today they just don't have what it takes. There are too many levels of authority within the building companies. They have a president, a vice-president and many other levels. We had formed an exceptional group of engineers. There was an enthusiasm in this group that was unequalled anywhere. We worked every day until midnight. On Sundays we quit at six p.m., so we knew we had a 'weekend.' "

Unfortunately, the Allison people, at their plant in Indianapolis, failed to deliver the engine for the new fighter test airplane. It was a further eighteen days before it arrived for installation in the airframe. The Flight Test Division of North American then prepared the necessary instrumentation and on October 11, 1940 the aircraft,

NA-73X, was given initial run-up tests.

Initial flight testing began on Saturday, October 26, and continued until November 20. On that day the test pilot neglected to put the fuel valve on "reserve" and ran out of fuel after fifteen minutes of flight. He was forced to put the precious prototype down on a freshly-plowed field. As he landed, the wheels dug into the soft ground, causing the airplane to flip on its back. The pilot was uninjured, but NA-73X was badly damaged and required a time-consuming rebuild.

Schmued's team decided to have the second airplane on the shop line—which was actually scheduled to be the first production airplane—prepared for flight test, so as not to delay the gathering of the critical test data needed immediately if the new plane was to be produced on time.

Before NA-73X was flown for the first time, the British ordered an additional 300 planes, making a new total buy of 620. A letter from the British purchasing authority to North American on December 9, 1940 referred to the fighter as "Mustang," its new official name.

In August 1941, the first Mustang I, AG346, to be accepted for delivery to the British, was crated and shipped via the Panama Canal from Long Beach, California, to England, where it was assembled and test-flown on November 11. During August and September, the U.S. Army had also accepted several of the new planes, the first being designated XP-51. It was flown to Wright Field in Ohio for additional testing and evaluation, while at the same time the North American Flight Test Division continued testing two examples at the California facility.

All 620 examples of the British order were completed and delivered by July 1942, and Mustang Is were in service with fifteen RAF-

Army Co-operation squadrons by December. They were used primarily for reconnaissance on low-level cross-Channel dashes in which they shot up German trains, barges, and troop concentrations, and did valuable photo reconaissance work. The RAF pilots flying these Mustang Is liked the airplanes and thought them easily "the best American fighters to have reached Britain." Compared with the Spitfire VB, the Mustang was faster up to 25,000 feet and had twice its range. However, the Spit VB could go much higher, had a better rate of climb and turn rate, and owed its high-altitude superiority to its Rolls-Royce Merlin engine. When Rolls-Royce test pilot Ronald Harker was invited by the RAF to Duxford airfield near Cambridge on April 30, 1942 to fly the Mustang I, he was impressed by the American fighter's handling qualities, fuel capacity (three times that of the Spitfire V), and by the positioning of the guns in the wing, which he felt gave greater accuracy. His report to the RAF Air Fighting Development Unit on the Mustang's general performance was very positive. It was in that report that Harker suggested that a really special fighter might result if this exceptional airframe were to be combined with the proven and fuel-efficient Rolls-Royce Merlin engine. However, the report, and his subsequent lobbying of officials in his company and in the Air Ministry, met with little initial enthusiasm. Few of them wanted anything to do with an American-built aircraft. Nonetheless, Harker was ultimately able to convince senior people at Rolls-Royce that his idea of mating the Merlin to the Mustang was not only likely to result in a wonderful new weapon against the Nazis, but would also produce a great deal of new engine business for Rolls. Influential executives at the engine maker then

persuaded the RAF to provide three Mustangs for Merlin installation at the R-R Hucknall factory.

Next came a series of modifications, conversions, and redesigns of the cowling and the cooling system, along with other detail changes which, in the end, produced a Merlin 65-powered Mustang designated Mark X, a highly successful realization of Ronnie Harker's inspiration.

Rolls-Royce sent its performance and factory installation data on the Mk X to North American's design staff in California, who began preliminary adaptive designs to incorporate the marvellous Merlin into production-line Mustangs. Agreements were reached with the Packard Motor Car Company and Continental Motors for the mass production in the United States of the V-12 Merlin under license from Rolls, to supplement British production of the engine. Among the many changes required by the Merlin-Mustang installation was the move to an enormous 11-foot 2-inch Hamilton Standard hydromatic propeller.

By November 1942, General "Hap" Arnold had been convinced of the promise of the rapidly developing Mustang and had ordered more than 2,200 of the new fighters for the U.S. Army Air Corps. By this time, North American was inundated with orders for its B-25 Mitchell bomber and AT-6 Texan trainer, as well as for the Mustang, now designated P-51B. It began to construct expanded manufacturing facilities at Inglewood, a new plant for Mustang production in Dallas (the plane built there was designated P-51C but was identical to the Inglewood product), and yet another new plant at Tulsa, Oklahoma.

Mustang production at the North American plants proceeded smoothly after initial delivery delays of Merlin engines from Packard had been overcome. Performance testing of the early Merlin production airplanes proved the brilliance of Ronald Harker's idea. The new plane had a top speed of 441 mph, more than fifty mph faster than the Allison-powered Mustang, and it showed greatly improved performance in all other categories as well.

The first American fighter group in the European Theater of Operations to get the P-51B was the 354th FG, based in England at Greenham Common in Berkshire. Their initial Mustangs arrived on November 11, 1943. There the new fighters underwent field modification to ready them for combat operations. These included the addition of external additional fuel capacity in the form of droppable aluminum and compressed paper tanks. Some Mustangs also received an eighty-five–U.S.-gallon fuel tank in the fuselage right behind the pilot's

seat as a field modification, a change that became a production standard with the last 550 P-51Bs.

The Mustang encountered teething problems as it took on its primary long-range bomber escort role. Prolonged high-altitude operation soon resulted in the freezing of certain oils and greases, oxygen starvation, ice buildup on windscreens, coolant loss and the resultant engine overheating condition, fouled spark plugs, and jammed ammunition belts during high-G maneuvers. All of these bugs were ultimately fixed, most of them in the field by airplane crew chiefs. Field representatives from North American passed information about the various problems and fixes employed by the group ground crews back to the company and modifications were soon incorporated into the factory production line planes.

With the arrival of General James "Jimmy" Doolittle as the new com-

mander of the Eighth Air Force early in January 1944, some of the escort fighters were released from their full-time commitment to the bombers they were shepherding and were, for the first time, given the freedom to attack and destroy German fighters both before and after the Germans attacked the American bombers. Now the Mustang began to show what it had and could do. More American fighter groups were being equipped with the slender, agile aircraft, and, by March 3, when Mustangs escorted bombers of the Eighth all the way to Berlin, a trip of more than a thousand miles, the Americans knew that they finally had the long-range fighter they needed to defeat the German air force.

In its continuing effort to improve their already splendid air weapon, North American modified a P-51B from its Inglewood line to carry a "bubble" or "teardrop" canopy for

A Sea Harrier jump jet coming aboard HMS *Illustrious*.

greatly enhanced visibility. The canopy became the most recognizable feature of the next Mustang version, the P-51D, which also featured a strengthened airframe, a standard eighty-five-gallon fuselage fuel tank, a slightly modified cowling, a landing gear modification, wing armament standardized to be six .50 caliber Browning machine guns, and a V-1650-7 Packard Merlin engine of 1,695 hp (war emergency rating). These highly capable new D models were soon arriving at the American fighter groups in England and other war theaters.

The widespread availability of this newest and most highly-evolved Mustang gave the U.S. fighter groups a new target priority. If enemy aircraft could be successfully attacked and destroyed while still parked on their airfields, if their hangars, runways, and other airfield facilities could be rendered unusable, the Allied cause in the air war could be considerably advanced. General Doolittle was quick to support this new priority, releasing some P-51 squadrons to hit the enemy airfields and other surface targets and the Mustangs proved extremely effective in this added role. For the remainder of the war, significantly more Mustangs were lost to German ground fire than to aerial combat. The German Luftwaffe was efficient in the defense of their airfields, which were heavily ringed with antiaircraft weapons. The Mustangs were particularly vulnerable to hits in the cooling system and many were shot to pieces or brought down by shrapnel strikes to the radiator or cooling tubes while attacking the enemy aerodromes. But in spite of the increased losses to ground fire, the Mustang was considered quite effective in the ground-attack role, if less so than the heavier, radial-engined P-47 Thunderbolt.

As dominant as the P-51 had become in the skies over German-occupied Europe, its pilots were soon facing fearsome new technology from the other side. Jet and rocket-propelled fighters, the Me 262 and Me 163 respectively, were appearing with increased frequency in the enemy's defense of the Reich effort, and their performance—though limited and erratic—was startling and devastating. They went through the American bomber formations like a hot knife through butter, often destroying two or more heavy bombers in a single pass. But while the speed and performance of the Me 262, for example, were considerably superior to that of the Mustang, they were never available to the Germans in numbers great enough to overcome the powerful presence of the P-51s.

In the Pacific theater of the war, the new Boeing B-29 Superfortress long-range heavy bombers, with their massive incendiary loads, were starting to bring the fury and terror of the man-made firestorm to the Japanese home islands, which were fiercely defended by the enemy fighter force. This was the supreme test for the P-51D. It was required to operate in the vital escort role, flying with the B-29s over thousands of miles of lonely and cruel sea. An often quoted reference to the early Superfortresses was "three turning, one burning" due to their inclination toward developing engine problems. The Mustangs freqently had to shepherd the big bombers, which were crippled by mechanical failure, while simultaneously fending off the attacks of Japanese fighters on the hunt for easy pickings among the American heavies. Still, the B-29s efficiently practiced the fire-bombing technique on the more than sixty key Japanese target cities, all but burning them to a fine ash by

the end of the war. The Superforts were accompanied to and from their objectives by P-51s, which operated mainly from a precious little SeaBee-built airfield on the small island of Iwo Jima. Flying from Iwo, the Mustangs took final control of the airspace over Japan, maintaining it until the atomic bombing of Hiroshima and Nagasaki and the end of the Pacific war in August 1945.

The Mustang continued to be developed through a succession of variants until the end of the war and was, without question, one of the most successful and highly-regarded fighter planes in the history of aviation. By the end of the war, Mustangs of the USAAF, the RAF, and other Allied air forces had destroyed nearly 5,000 enemy aircraft in the European theater alone. The combat life of the plane was extended in the Korean War in 1950, in Arab-Israeli wars, and in other conflicts, serving with many different air forces.

More than 200 Mustangs are still flown today worldwide—careful, loving restorations of proud enthusiasts who continue to appreciate the charms and performance of an airplane that many believe contributed more to the winning of World War II than any other.

Eighty-five-year-old Ed Schmued, the kind, modest, quiet designer of the Mustang, died of heart failure on Saturday, June 1, 1985. His body was cremated and, at the request of his wife, Christel, his ashes were flown from Los Angeles International Airport in Inglewood where his Mustang was conceived, out to sea where they were released. His last flight took place in a Mustang.

At seventeen, Cecil Lewis earned the wings on his Royal Flying Corps tunic and, with a total of thirteen flying hours to his credit, left for France to join No 56 Squadron in February 1916. He quickly learned about air fighting and about the fighter planes of the day. "At Martlesham, I realized a long-cherished ambition—to fly scouts. My attempt with the Bristol Bullet at St. Omer in the spring of the previous year had been disastrous. Since then no opportunity had come along; but one day the Sopwith Triplane arrived at Martlesham Heath for tests.

"Of all the machines, the Triplane remains in my memory as the best— for the actual pleasure of flying—that I ever took up. It was so beautifully balanced, so well-mannered, so feather-light on the stick, and so comfortable and warm. It had what was then a novel feature, an adjustable tail plane to trim the machine fore and aft. Set correctly, with the throttle about three-quarters open, the Tripe would loop, hands off, indefinitely. Not for this, but for its docility, the lack of all effort needed to fly it, and yet its instantaneous response to the lightest touch, it remains my favorite. Other machines were faster, stronger, had better climb or vision; but none was so friendly as the Tripe. After it I never wanted to fly anything but scout again, and on active service I never did."

Like most radical new designs, the Vought F4U Corsair was born with a lot of inherent problems. More than a hundred separate modifications were required just to correct problems with lateral stability and aileron control. But the United States Navy knew it had something very special when, in 1940, the XF4U-1 prototype achieved more than 400 mph in level flight testing, the first American combat aircraft to do so. That early test airplane had just been rebuilt after suffering a devas-

The cockpit of a Focke-Wulf Fw 190 fighter, the finest propeller-driven German fighter of the Second World War.

tating crash-landing during a previous test flight.

When Vought was developing the Corsair, they chose to employ the new and highly promising Pratt & Whitney R-2800 engine to power their new bird. It was a brilliant match, even though both engine and prototype aircraft were plagued by teething troubles that took up a lot of development time. In the process, General "Hap" Arnold, who had been watching the progress of the P & W powerplant, was so impressed that he told the engine maker to drop its work developing a liquid-cooled engine for the U.S. Army and concentrate entirely on the R-2800 and other radial aircraft engines.

The Corsair featured a unique new inverted "bent" gull wing design made necessary by a very large thirteen-foot-four-inch propeller that transferred the power of the big engine. Such a large propeller mounted on an airplane with a conventional wing would have resulted in an unacceptably high angle of attack in landing and takeoff. The bent wing brought other advantages to the new fighter. Vision from the cockpit was improved, and the folding point of the wing meant that the plane took up less room on board a carrier, where aircraft storage space was limited. The inverted gull wing also offered a reduced drag factor, further adding to the Corsair's fine performance.

The combat record of the Corsair is legendary. It destroyed 2,140 enemy aircraft during World War II against a loss of 935 Corsairs (190 in aerial combat, 350 from antiaircraft fire, 230 from other causes, and 165 in crash landings). A further 692 were lost on non-operational missions.

The Corsair was built by Chance Vought (7,829), Brewster (735), and Goodyear (4,017). The U.S. employed the majority of the Corsairs, while Great Britain operated 2,020 and New Zealand 430.

According to Captain Alan Leahy, RN (Ret), his favorite aircraft was the one he happened to be flying at the time: "What you had to do was identify the aircraft's good points and then build your tactics around them. The Corsair was rough and tough, but in no way could you think of entering a one-on-one dogfight with a Zero. Get in quick and get out quick was the preferred method of attack. The Sea Fury was the second fastest propeller-driven aircraft in the world. Highly maneuverable, it was a delight to fly and fight. It would outmaneuver any jet and the MiGs in Korea soon learned not to try and mix it, and used the fast-in-fast-out philosophy. The Sea Hornet was the fastest propeller-driven aircraft. It had a high rate of climb, but it could not outrun the Sea Fury. The Sea Hornet could mix it with jets, but that was never put to the test in war. Ideal as a fleet fighter, it had a long range and endurance, and with the cockpit right up front between the two engines it was perfect for deck landings, giving the pilot an excellent view of any impending accident."

No combat plane is perfect in all respects. Knowing an aircraft's limitations is as fundamental to combat survivability as knowing its capabilities. The most serious limitation of the P-47 Thunderbolt fighter was its comparatively slow rate of climb. It was, however, a remarkably rugged airplane, armed with a wing-mounted battery of eight .50 caliber Browning machine guns. Underwing rockets and bombs could add to its firepower for the ground-attack role. It was the biggest single-seat, single-engined Allied fighter of World War II, and its shape soon earned it the nickname Jug, with its bulbous front and tapering fuselage it certainly resembled a milk jug.

If the Thunderbolt did not climb very well, it could surely dive. Its pilots attributed this characteristic to what they called the milk-bottle effect. Gravity and the massive Pratt & Whitney Wasp R-2800 radial engine driving a huge four-blade propeller made its dive impressive by any standard. The P-47's great size though, made the first impression on pilots new to it: "Gee," said one Spitfire veteran as he looked into a Thunderbolt cockpit for the first time, "you could walk around in there!"

The Thunderbolt was more than just big; it was an ace-maker. In it, many Eighth and Ninth Air Force pilots achieved that status. It was the airplane with which the high-achieving 4th and 56th Fighter Groups first became famous. Once the early engine and radio problems common to the aircraft had been overcome, the Thunderbolt became an outstanding fighter—appreciated by its pilots

The employee badge of a lady war worker in WWII; right: A factory-fresh Lockheed P-38 on the company ramp at the Burbank plant.

and by the German air force.

In the 1990s a magnificently restored P-47 was still being flown regularly by Stephen Grey of the Fighter Collection, at Duxford, Cambridgeshire, England: "Settle into the cockpit and space plus comfort prevail. Start the 2800 engine and it begins to feel like a class act. Taxi to the hold and if feels like a beautifully damped Mack truck. At run-up it purrs rather than barks.

"Put the hammer down for take-off and there is no kick in the back or dart for the weeds. It runs straight and true—if sedately.

"Put the wheels in the wings and it turns into a crisp-handling fighter, with beautiful ailerons, outstanding controls, great visibility and a sensation of pedigree.

"True, it does not climb with the best of them, but stuff the nose toward the greenery and the airspeed indicator will wind to the stop and stay there faster than other prop fighters that I have flown. Circuit work, landing and ground handling are docile and beautifully mannered.

"Fortunately, or regrettably, I have not had to fight in the Jug. However, from a little 'arm wrestling' with others behind the hangar I know that the Jug could fight incredibly well, if differently. If I were able to transpose myself back to the 1940s and had a choice, I feel my survival instincts would tell me to choose the Jug, but my competitive instincts would tell me only to fight on my terms with a lot of airspace underneath me.

"The sheer rugged, technical quality of the airplane is its charm, the handling a joy. When I climb out and walk away, I always find myself looking back at the P-47 with affection— what a character."

"My personal favorite fighter is the F-16. I flew it for fourteen years. It is small, agile and powerful. It is also very easy to fly, wonderful for low-level aerobatics and a fine weapons platform, with perfect visibility."
—Gidi Livni, formerly a colonel in the Israeli Air Force

Pilot Officer Nick Berryman of No 276 Squadron, RAF, was a Hurricane man. Although he never flew one operationally, he remembered the airplane vividly: "Friday, 16 October 1942. Flew Master for twenty minutes, then pushed off in a Hurri. Very careful indeed. Twenty minutes for cockpit check, which I carried out about five times. Eventually ready to go. Got off OK, but unable to find undercart lever. Terrible moments expecting to spin in any minute. Aircraft bucking about all over the place. Climbed to 1,000 feet, then selecting 'wheels down' found myself at 1,700 feet. Forgot radio procedure completely and unable to remember call sign. Suddenly, a crosswind coming in to land. All became calm and she came in as gentle as a bird. Now, at long last, a Hurricane has flown me.

"Not exactly a macho way of describing one's first flight in a fighter aircraft, but that is exactly how it was. Over a beer in the bar that night I probably said, 'Hurricanes? A piece of cake.'"

Like so many Hurricane pilots, Berryman learned to love and respect the airplane: "Give it half a chance and it would do its best to safeguard the pilot. There was little or no swing on takeoff and in flight it was comfortable. Apart from the undercarriage, all the tits and knobs were in the right places. It was delightfully steady in all attitudes and steep turns were a joy. So too, were aerobatics, which I could carry out more accurately on Hurricanes than Spits, which I tended to over-aileron. I'm told that fifteen degrees of flap milked down in a dogfight situation would leave your tail-chasing adversary wondering why he could not stay with you.

"Landing was no problem. One bounce it would absorb without a murmur. Two bounces it would

remind you to be careful, and I never saw anyone bounce three times. If you did that, it would take over and drop fairly straight in on its wide legs. Without doubt, the Hurricane helped me to a state of proficiency I would never have achieved on any other fighter. It was a winner all the way. And yes, the airplane was probably more capable than many of the pilots who flew it."

Wing Commander Geoffrey Page flew it in combat: "In the Hurricane we knew that the Me 109 could out-dive us, but not out-turn us. With that knowledge one obviously used the turning maneuver rather than trying to beat the man at the game in which he was clearly superior. With a 109 sitting behind you, you'd stay in a really tight turn and after a few turns the positions would be reversed and you'd be on his tail. In short, I'd say that the Hurricane was a magnificent airplane to go to war in."

The Fw 190A-8 was the favorite mount of Oscar Boesch, German air force (Ret), a former feldwebel of *Sturm Staffel 1*, IV/JG3 "Udet". In his career as a fighter pilot, Boesch was credited with destroying six B-17s, two B-24s, one P-51, one Spitfire, and eight Russian aircraft. He experienced four bail-outs, four crash-landings, two midair collisions, and for three days was a prisoner of the Russians until he managed to escape: "We considered the Fw 190 superior to the Mustang and Thunderbolt. The Fw 190's robust construction and its flight characteristics made it a great fighter. It had excellent handling qualities and maneuvered superbly. It had two fuselage-mounted 13mm machine guns and a 20mm cannon in each wing root as well as a 30mm Mk 108 cannon in each wing.

"I never had a problem dogfighting

with any opponent. The only fighter that might have had an edge on maneuverability was the Spitfire, with the Mustang a close second. The big air-cooled BMW 801D engine provided the power, and in some variants we even had extra horsepower provided by a booster. The large radial engine also provided much protection for the pilot and could take severe punishment before it seized from being shot up.

"Our tactic against the bombers was to attack from behind regardless of the deadly defensive fire. If we couldn't down the bomber with a firing pass, then we were to ram. All *Sturm Staffel* pilots signed a declaration to do our duty to the utmost of our ability. About the ramming tactic, this was always considered a last and final option for downing the enemy. The decision to ram was left up to the individual. It was a last-ditch method to stem the bomber tide, but at the same time we knew we were of greater value to our country alive than dead. The Fw 190 was known throughout the Luftwaffe as the *Würger*, which means Butcherbird. In *Sturm Staffel 1* we called it the *Sturmbock*, which equates to Ram. We thought this an appropriate name for the aircraft."

Captain Eric Brown, RN (Ret), served as a Fleet Air Arm fighter pilot in World War II and in January 1944 became the Royal Navy's chief test pilot at the Royal Aircraft Establishment, Farnborough. There he flew many captured German aircraft and, at war's end, his position and his command of the German language led to his interrogating some of Germany's most successful aircraft designers, including Messerschmitt, Heinkel, and Tank. He was designated officer in charge of German Aircraft Reception at Farnborough, and in his

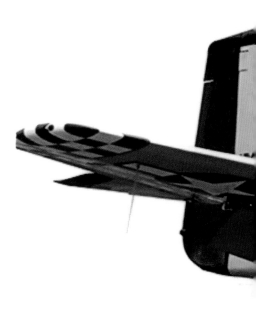

This Mustang performed in air shows at Duxford for years until it sadly was destroyed in a midair collision there. The pilot was able to bail out and was unhurt in the incident.

time there he flew fifty-five different types of German World War II aircraft: "If asked to nominate the most formidable combat aircraft to evolve in World War II, I would unhesitatingly propose Messerschmitt's Me 262. I say 'unhesitatingly' advisedly, despite having flown the Spitfire in virtually all its variants, the Mosquto, the Lancaster, the Mustang and even Mitsubishi's Zero-Sen—all warplanes that might be considered as contenders for this accolade.

"The Me 262 was a fantastic

aeroplane from several aspects, and its eleventh hour début in the Götterdämmerung of Germany's Third Reich provided as dramatic a movement as any the great Wagner himself could have composed. In this case, however, the 'composer' was one Professor Willy Messerschmitt, whose Bf 109 fighter, after blooding over Spain, had provided most of the vertebrae of the German air force's spinal column throughout the entire war. The same fertile brain had given birth to the Bf 110 and the Me 410,

both very useful twin-engined combat aircraft, but its *piece de résistance* was unquestionably the Me 262, which was both turbojet-driven and swept-winged—a truly startling combination in 1944.

"I was immediately struck by its beautiful yet sinister lines, which reminded me of those of a shark. I was very keen to get airborne in this aircraft, but interrogation of some of the German air force pilots led our team to proceed with some caution.

"My first cursory glance around the

cockpit of the Me 262 had revealed what was, by 1945 standards, a complex but neat layout. The dashboard carried the flight instruments on the left and the engine gauges on the right. The left console carried the throttles, fuel cocks, trimmers, ancillary controls and their emergencies, while the right had the electronics, starters and radio equipment. All this compared pretty closely with British practice.

"Once the rigamarole of starting had been completed, and assuming that both engines were functioning, the process of taxiing could begin.

"The view from the cockpit was excellent, and every upper part of the aircraft was within the pilot's field of vision. The main wheelbrakes were operated, as on all German aircraft, by toe action, and the Me 262 embodied the somewhat odd feature of a hand-operated nosewheel brake, which, I assume, was needed when the aircraft was fully loaded, German brakes never seeming too positive in their action.

"The takeoff preparations were simple enough. At full power fumes or smoke invariably penetrated the cockpit, and, as the canopy had to be closed for takeoff, the sensation was, to say the least, disturbing. The nosewheel was raised at 100 mph, and the aircraft pulled gently off at 124 mph.

"The takeoff run was long, and the aircraft gave one the feeling that it was underpowered, as indeed was the contemporary Meteor I.

"Our interest in the Me 262 at RAE Farnborough was threefold. First,

we were intrigued to discover if the performance really did match the capabilities claimed by the Germans; second, we were anxious to discover the behavior of the swept-wing configuration at high Mach numbers; and, third, we wanted to know if this aircraft provided a good gun platform. We soon ascertained that the German performance figures were by no means extravagant, but the high Mach performance must, of course, be related to the contemporary state of the art, to use an Americanism.

"The normal range of flight characteristics from aerobatic manoevres to the stall revealed the Me 262 as a very responsive and docile aeroplane, leaving one with a confident impression of a first-class combat aircraft for both fighter and ground attack roles.

"The Me 262's landing run was long and was always accompanied by that unpleasant suspicion of fading brakes that one had with all German aircraft of the period.

"The Me 262 [was] variously known as the *Schwalbe* and *Sturmvogel*,

but whatever the appelation it was in my view unquestionably the foremost warplane of its day; a hard hitter which outperformed anything that we had immediately available but which, fortunately for the Allies, was not available to the German air force in sufficient numbers to affect drastically the course of events in the air over Europe. It was a pilot's aeroplane which had to be flown and not just heaved into the air. Basically underpowered and fitted with engines sufficiently lacking in reliability to keep the adrenaline flowing, it was thoroughly exciting to fly, and particularly so in view of its lack of an ejector seat. I was reminded vividly of this aircraft when I first flew the F-4 Phantom some twenty years later. This later generation U.S. aircraft offered its pilot that same feeling of sheer exhilaration, but the Phantom possessed the added attractions of safety and reliability which perhaps kept the pulse at a somewhat lower tempo than it attained when flying the Me 262 in those now-distant days of 1945."

The de Havilland Mosquito was known as "the wooden wonder" and was among the most unusual and versatile aircraft of the war years; right: Ruined Me 262 jet fighters in a bombed German production facility near the end of the Second World War.

Neither the Royal Navy nor the U.S. Navy had the front-line fighter they needed in the early part of World War II. The Corsair was on order and promised the qualities both naval air arms required, but they did not know if the new Chance Vought plane would perform up to its specifications, and so the Americans decided to buy some insurance. The navy purchasing people asked Grumman to build an improved and updated version of the Wildcat, and in the effort something entirely new and much better resulted—the XF6F-1, later called the Hellcat. Designed by Leroy Grumman and William Schwendler, the prototype was first flown in June 1942 at Grumman's Bethpage facility on Long Island, New York. That first airplane left a lot to be desired. It was underpowered by 25 percent. The first engine was replaced with a Pratt & Whitney R-2800, which fixed the speed and rate-of-climb problems. But the plane had a tendency to flutter in high-speed dives and it required too much trim adjustment between flaps-up and flaps-down. These and other early problems were corrected, and Grumman moved rapidly to set up a new production line for the Hellcat.

Production of the new fighter actually progressed faster than completion of the factory housing the assembly line. The new production version, the F6F-3, was given an R-2800-10 engine rated at 2,000 hp at 2,700 rpm.

The Hellcat was sturdy and built to take the shock of carrier landing and the punishment of enemy fire. With six .50 caliber Colt-Browning machine guns, and 400 rounds for each gun, it could dish it out as well. Hellcats were delivered to U.S. Navy fighter squadrons and to the Royal Navy in quantity during 1943, and they immediately showed their worth in action.

A Republic P-47 Thunderbolt fighter. The type was extremely effective in the hands of pilots with the 56th and 78th Fighter Groups.

The F6F was the first naval fighter of the war to meet the Japanese Zero on equal terms. Excepting tight turns, the Hellcat gave at least as well as it got. Its toughness made it popular with Allied naval aviators, if not with the opposition who now had something substantial to worry about. The Cat was also popular with mechanics and repair person-nel. Her engine and systems were easily accessible. Maintenance and repairs were normally done quickly and with little fuss or strain.

As early as August 1940, General Claire Chennault was warning the U.S. military about the startlingly superior performance of the Japanese Zero. He was talking about the model 11 Zero. By 1942, the best aircraft of U.S. Navy fighter squadrons were still being shot to pieces by the Zero, now the model 21. In the Zero, the Japanese had a battle-tested, proven fighter of impressive perfor-mance and capability. In it they were confident and ready to go to war.

As early as November 1937, the Imperial Japanese Navy knew what

guns, a requirement that both manufacturers saw as unrealistic, and Nakajima pulled out of the competition to build the new plane. The contract went to Mitsubishi, who agreed to try to solve the gun problem. But it turned out that Nakajima had been right and, in the end, the armament requirement was modified.

An initially underpowered prototype Zero was completed in a little over a year using a tough new lightweight alloy called Extra-Super Duralumin (ESD).

Testing in the spring of 1939 identified some relatively minor problems which were soon resolved, and on September 14 the Zero was accepted by the Imperial Japanese Navy as the A6M1 carrier fighter. The new armament consisted of two 20mm cannon in the wings and two 7.7mm machine guns set in the upper cowling and firing through the propeller. She was good—but she was going to be better.

Mitsubishi designers were waiting for a new engine, the 925-hp Nakajima NK1C Sakae 12, to pass its naval acceptance so they could install it in what was now the A6M2 Zero. The new engine gave the already impressive plane significantly improved performance, and the new weapon presented the Allies with a staggering challenge until well into 1943 when the Hellcat and the Corsair arrived.

it needed in a future first-line fighter plane, and gave its requirements to the Mitsubishi and Nakajima aircraft companies. The navy wanted a fighter with a top speed of at least 310 mph, outstanding maneuverability, the ability to climb to 10,000 feet in 3.5 minutes, and a better range than that of any existing fighter. The armament had to be two cannon and two machine

Some years ago I was standing near a display in the World War II wing of the Smithsonian's National Air and Space Museum in Washington, DC. Next to me were three men in the uniform of the German air force. Two were in their early twenties. The third man was clearly a very senior officer of many years' service. We began a conversation about the aircraft we were all observing, a Messerschmitt

Me 109G, and I asked the elderly officer if he had flown the type. He told me he had flown it in the war, and I asked his opinion of the machine. He said he thought it an excellent fighter, every bit as good and capable as most marks of the Spitfire, and better than many of its other opponents. He was silent for moment before commenting that he had lost many friends, fellow 109 pilots whose aircraft had been shot up in aerial combat: "In most cases, they died because they were unable to get out of the tiny cockpit in the few seconds left to them before it was too late—they had been trapped."

The Me 109, known officially in German plans and technical documents as the Bf 109, began life in 1934 when the German air ministry let contracts for prototypes of a new single-seat monoplane fighter to four aircraft manufacturers: Arado, Heinkel A.G., Focke Wulf Flugzeugwerke, and Bayerische Flugzeugwerk (Bf). The latter's Bf 109 prevailed in the competition, which was influenced by German military intelligence reports from Britain. The new fighter offered advanced controls, an enclosed cockpit, automatic leading-edge slats to provide extra lift on take-off, and slotted flaps and ailerons. Bf's chief designer, Professor Willy Messerschmitt, had produced a very advanced aircraft, but it was a long way from achieving wide acceptance. It was something less than a hit with the experimental test pilots who experienced a variety of failures with all ten of the initial aircraft ordered for trial at the Rechlin Experimental Establishment.

By July 1937, most of the bugs had been worked out of the 109. At that point, Dr. Josef Göbbels and Hermann Goering decided that the time was right for a practical demonstration of what Göbbels had called "the wonder plane." The German air force re-equipped two *staffeln* with twenty-four new Bf 109Bs and sent them off to fight in the Spanish Civil War as the Condor Legion. In full production now, the 109 attracted a lot of attention from the international press covering the war in Spain, and much of what they wrote and photographed was extremely bad press for the plane, the plane maker, and for Germany. More than 1,500 109s had been lost before the Spanish War in takeoff and landing accidents owing to excessive torque; historical records show that many more were lost during the Civil War itself. Subsequent C and D versions of the 109 were essentially exercises in additional problem-solving. But by the time of the Battle of Britain in the summer of 1940, the E model was out in strength and proved itself to be one of the finest fighter aircraft of World War II.

The Bf or Me 109E was powered by an 1,100 hp Daimler-Benz 601A

After the war most of the remaining fighters, bombers, transports, and trainers of the American Air Force, Navy and Marine Corps were brought back to the United States for a period in storage at one of several airplane graveyards. Some were preserved for possible further use, some were sold to "friendly foreign governments," and many were chopped up, melted down into aluminum ingots, and reused. These examples are Curtiss P-40 fighters.

engine with direct fuel injection, an enormous advantage over its Spitfire and Hurricane opponents whose Rolls-Royce Merlin engines tended to cut out when flying inverted. Where the odds changed in favor of the RAF was in the matter of the limited flying time of the 109 from its bases in western Europe. It had a maximum

of one and a half hours in the air when escorting bombers to attack targets in England, with only about ten minutes of fighting time over the target area. The fighters of the RAF were defending and fighting over their own land and could easily land, refuel, re-arm, and be back in the air to fight again as many as five or six times in a day. Many German fighter pilots in the Battle found themselves running on empty on their return trips, and getting their feet wet in the English Channel.

Between 1936 and the end of the war in Europe, Messerschmitt produced more than 33,000 Bf 109s through many different marks and changes in power, armament, and performance. The plane operated in various campaigns including western Europe, Britain, Africa, and Russia.

For much of the war Günther Rall flew 109s in Russia: "The war had been raging in Russia for two years. It was a different one than in the west—ideologically motivated, brutal, and destructive—in a battle where no quarter was given. After my crash following an aerial fight on November 28, 1941, I was seriously injured with three broken vertebrae in the spine, paralysis and head injuries. German tank drivers had pulled me from the wreckage of my downed Me 109 at a freezing temperature of minus forty degrees Centigrade. Following nine months of rehabilitation in military hospitals in Bucharest and Vienna, I was declared fit and ready for action. Back with my squadron, VIII/JG52, I was just in time for the push to the Caucasus mountains, the retreat and new action at Stalingrad at Christmas 1942. Then more retreats. Action on the Crimea and Kuban bridgehead. I then received additional treatment for my paralysis in a Vienna field hospital. There a telegram reached me

calling me back to the front as the new group commander of III/JG52. Then to action at Bjulgorod over the Pocket of Kursk. I reached my fighter group shortly before the attack started—the biggest tank battle of all time. It was summer 1943 and we were flying as many as five missions a day.

"One day in the late afternoon I was flying with my adjutant as wingman in pursuit over the Pocket. I was looking from west to east and spotted two aircraft silhouettes flashing against huge cumulus clouds lit up by the late afternoon sun. With full throttle I closed behind the two radial-engined fighters and fixed the left one in my sight. He did not see me. I could have shot, but I was in doubt. A few days earlier a Fw 190 group was moved to that part of the front. I had never seen an Fw 190 in the air. Were the two in front of me Fw 190s? With additional speed I pulled up to the left and looked down. I could see the red star and the dark green color—Russians!

"A Lagg 5. Too late to pass him . . . then I would be the hunted. So, I closed and attacked from above at a short distance and shot. After a short burst of fire I pulled out of a dive and my Me 109 stalled. After a hit and a bang—which I will never forget as long as I live—the right wing of the Lagg flew by. She was spinning out of control below. My engine was vibrating as if it was breaking up. At an altitude of 4,000 metres, I was more or less heading towards the German lines. I found a meadow and, in a gentle turn, came to a landing with the gear down. After landing, a mechanic showed me a metre cut on the underside of the me 109. I had been lucky to survive."

Pilot Officer Leo Nomis, formerly with No 71 (Eagle) Squadron, RAF, in World War II, flew the Me 109 for the Israelis in 1948–49: "It was all they could get at the time. Got them from the Czechs. Nobody else would sell the Israelis anything. Had to smuggle them in. They modified the 109Gs and they were real tricky to fly, with a lot more accidents. Didn't lose any in air-to-air. Lost about five to ground fire. The problem was, you had to go to Czechoslovakia to check out on them because you couldn't just check out on 'em like you would a regular fighter. They had a helluva lot of real dangerous habits. They had changed the center of gravity on it. They changed the engine and the whole airframe. Then they put a 211 Jumo engine in it, which was a Ju 88 engine. They had to change it from one side to the other and the prop went the other way and it had a helluva torque on it. You'd be takin' off into the tents and the jeeps. And then, when it landed, it had a helluva swing on it if you didn't catch it right away. It would groundloop on you. In Israel we used to call it 'the battle of the Messerschmitts."

RAF pilot Tony Mead flew the F-86 Sabre in the postwar years at Wildenwrath, Germany, where the 2nd Tactical Air Force had established a small conversion unit to which RAF pilots went for their first experience on the Sabre: "When we arrived in early 1954, there were some dog-eared copies of the Pilot's Notes, several laid-back Flight Lieutenant instructors who went through the notes in an appropriately relaxed manner, took us to the aircraft, helped us to strap in and, leaning into the cockpit actually started the GE J47 engine for us 'because otherwise you'll just burn the back off the bloody thing.' Jet engines of the time had very simple fuel systems and start-up was very much a manual affair, fiddling with the throttle at minimum to try and achieve a fuel

A British icon, the Vickers-Supermarine Spitfire fighter is one of the most famous aircraft in history. Beloved by its pilots for its delightful handling and agility, it was produced in greater numbers than any other British aircraft of the Second World War. Through the course of the war, 22,351 Spitfires in twenty-two variants were built. Above and following are images of its construction at Castle Bromwich, Birmingham. More than fifty Spitfires are still airworthy.

flow compatible with a cool light-up, which was not easy. Once achieved, however, and with the engine stabilized at an appropriate level, the instructor would say simply 'See you when you get back.' There were, of course, no F-86 two-seaters in the RAF fleet.

"The cultural change to this completely American swept-wing transonic fighter from the British Meteors and Vampires that we had flown up to then was daunting. First, used as we were to sitting in our Vampires with our bottoms practically scraping on the runway, we now found ourselves sitting high in the air looking out at first floor level. Gone too was our nice, tidy standardized RAF instrument flying panel and in its place a bunch of dissimilar instruments arranged around the cockpit in apparent confusion—at least to our trained eye. The control column had so many knobs, nipples, buttons, and switches that, although an ergonomic marvel, it was grasped with some trepidation.

"Cleared by the tower, we taxied out of our dispersal using nosewheel steering for the first time in our lives, and it was pure delight. The marvelous steerability on the deck gave immediate confidence. With the Sabre now lined up on the runway, and unable to find any further excuse for delay, there was nothing for it but to open the throttle to maximum power and release the brakes. There followed a seemingly wild acceleration and before realizing it we were airborne, wings wagging furiously due to an aileron sensitivity never before experienced, and climbing away at a frightening rate. Almost at once and whilst cleaning up, the cockpit began filling rapidly with white smoke! Calling an immediate re-entry for 'HEAVY SMOKE IN COCKPIT!' provoked a prompt of laconic 'adjust conditioning control, port console, to warm,' which, once found and done, thank God, rapidly dispersed the cloud. It is strange how water vapour can smell so decidedly of burning.

"Most of us honestly admitted that for the first flight or so in the Sabre we were not really fully in control but, surprisingly, practically the entire RAF conversion program of all the 2nd TAF pilots to the F-86 was achieved without incident.

"Notwithstanding its complexities, this graceful and maneuverable aircraft rapidly became a much loved and respected mount with a reliability highly appreciated by the 'chaps.' It had its idiosyncrasies, of course, a propensity for engine over-temperaturing on start-up and a tendency to surge during anything but a most gentle throttle opening. It was, in fact, common practice on takeoff to open the

Women war workers at Castle Bromwich completing the Irish linen tail surfaces of the magnificent fighter plane; right: Fitting out a new Spitfire cockpit.

throttle fast, which frequently caused an engine surge. By easing off a bit and opening wide again, chasing the rumble up the quadrant, a clean 100 percent was then achieved. This enabled you to catch up with your leader, who never really gave you sufficient time to tuck in properly for a formation takeoff. The ground attack role was helped by the innovative wing slats. Unfortunately, they didn't help its performance as an interceptor day fighter at high altitude and so 'hard edges' were fitted. These, in turn, required a great deal more airspeed in the circuit and on finals which, sadly, led to one or two incidents.

"Firing the six Browning machine guns in unison made a tremendous noise, smell, and vibration, and the radar gunsight ranging ring leapt about furiously. Counting colored bullet holes in the 'rag' [target sleeve] later was, however, a great satisfaction. If there weren't any, the Squadron Commander was inclined to comment that 'a fighter pilot who can't shoot is a contradiction in terms'.

"The Sabre was a fine aircraft and gun platform, and allowed its pilot considerable latitude. Flying it gave us the right to a special illuminated address and a lapel pin, certifying us to be a member in good standing of the Mach Busters Club, having exceeded the speed of sound in an F-86 Sabre Jet. However, this was achieved only by removing the wing tanks, climbing to 40,000 feet, rolling upside down, and pulling through to the vertical with the engine at full power. Diving vertically the airspeed built rapidly and, following some buffet at Mach .96—7, and a tendency to roll to port (easily corrected by gentle aileron), one slid through to Mach 1.03—4, at which point it was time to throttle back and start the pullout. This transonic capability was more of a curiosity than operationally useful,

but all of us stood just a wee bit taller after doing it for the first time."

Former USAF pilot John Lamb has more than 1,500 hours flying different versions of the F-4 Phantom: "The first thing that struck me about the F-4 was the size. I had been flying the A-37 for four years including 400 combat missions in Southeast Asia. The A-37 had great power / throttle response and turning capability, so

the transition to the Phantom was initially just a matter of getting used to the cockpit. I'll never forget the first time . . . taxiing onto the runway beside another F-4 for my first formation takeoff. What a big, powerful machine!

"In 1988, I was assigned to Spangdahlem AFB, Germany. As a reward for finding a highly sensitive and classified ALQ 131 jamming pod, which had fallen off one of our aircraft. I was given a chance to fly the F-4G 'Wild Weasel.' The Weasel mission was the most demanding thing I have ever attempted. It required air-to-air skills as well as conventional air-to-ground weapons delivery, in addition to the primary role of SAM [surface-to-air missile] killer. The co-ordination and trust required between the pilot and the electronic warfare officer (EWO) was of the highest order. The Weasel EWOs, and some of the backseaters I flew with in the Guard who had been former Navy/Marine RIOs [radar intercept officers], were some of the best and most respected aviators I have ever known."

U.S. Air Force Major Jonathan Holdaway had flown the F-15 Eagle for seven years prior to a more than three-year exchange tour with the Royal Air Force, where he flew the F3 Tornado with No 43 Squadron at RAF Leuchars in Scotland: "I love the F-15. That's my first love. Flying the Tornado with the Brits has been fun but deep in my heart I'll always be an Eagle driver. It's a great airplane to fly. It's optimized for one mission—to kill other airplanes. It's the greatest air-to-air fighter in history, the king of the skies. Talk to any country that flies them, particularly the Israelis. They have done some very, very good work with the F-15 in some of their conflicts. Combining our kills

Spitfire final assembly in the massive Castle Bromwich, Birmingham factory.

in Desert Storm with the kills the Israelis have had in their conflicts, its kill ratio is well over 100 to nothing, which no other airplane in the world can even come close to matching. It's an airplane designed by fighter pilots for fighter pilots and I just can't say enough good things about it.

"One of the big things I had to get used to in coming to this exchange with the RAF was the difference between the F-15 and the F3 Tornado. We do the same mission—shoot down and kill other airplanes. The Eagle is much easier to fly than the T-38, which is the airplane that we fly in training. The basic skills of taking off, flying from point A to point B, and landing in an F-15 are very simple. The airplane is very responsive to the pilot controls, with big, powerful engines out the back, and she'll do basically what you ask of her. The F-15 doesn't have all the fancy fly-by-wire systems and computers controlling the flight controls like some of the new airplanes. It's an airplane that was bridging the gap between the old-style fighters like the F-4 Phantom of Vietnam days and the new fighters with fly-by-wire computer-driven software systems. Flying the F-15 is very easy, but because it was designed for single-seat operation, the guy flying it and operating it has a relatively high workload.

"I have a guy in the back seat, a navigator, who controls the radar. He searches the sky, finds us targets, and then tells me where they are; he locks down to them with the radar and tells me when they are in range to shoot. He's also responsible for the navigation. The cockpit of the F3 Tornado is much less pilot-friendly than that of the F-15. The F3 is much harder to fly. Just getting the airplane from A to B and landing it is much more difficult than with the F-15. As I'm flying the Tornado, I have to be devoting part

of my concentration to keeping the thing airborne and flying where I want it to fly. The F-15 almost flies itself and I can concentrate more of my energy and attention on doing my mission—finding and destroying other airplanes.

"The F-15 was designed to fly high and relatively fast, to have a very good turn performance and a very high thrust-to-weight ratio, and to operate at medium to high altitudes. The F3 Tornado was designed as a follow-on to the GR1, which was designed as a low-altitude striker to penetrate the Warsaw Pact defenses back in the Cold War; to take out enemy airfields, strategic targets, that sort of thing. The F3, as a derivative of that design, shares a lot of that heritage. It has very high wing-loading with a very small wing. As a result, it doesn't turn very well. It bleeds energy quite quickly when you start maneuvering it hard. It doesn't have the same G capability that the F-15 has. It doesn't like medium to high-altitude flight because it was designed to fly down low. If, for instance, we are training against F-15s, F-16s, or F-18s, if we can drag them down into the low altitude arena, we can eliminate or reduce some of their advantages because that is where the F3 was designed to operate, low altitude within 1,000 feet of the ground. The F-15s and F-16s don't like to get down there with us because it eliminates some of their advantages, so they try to keep the fight up high and let their missiles come down and take us out at low altitude. But if we can defeat those long-range shots and get them to come down with us, then it's a little bit of a different fight. The bottom line, though, is that if an F3 is flown to its maximum performance and an F-15 is flown to its maximum performance, well, you know who is going to win that one. The F-15."

Chance-Vought F4-U Corsair fighters of the U.S. Navy on air patrol from the Essex-class carrier USS *Boxer.* Called "Whistling Death" by its Japanese opponents, the Corsair had an eleven-to-one kill ratio in WWII and served effectively in the Korean War as well.

A Mustang of the 356FG at Martlesham Heath
in Suffolk, England, photographed during
WWII.

GROUND GRIPPERS

MASTER SERGEANT MERLE OLMSTED, USAF (Ret), was a P-51 Mustang crew chief with the 357th Fighter Group at Leiston, England, in the Second World War. He recalled the daily grind on his fighter station: "Dawn had not yet broken through the cold and swirling mist at Leiston airfield on the coast of England's East Anglia bulge. On this January morning in 1945, many of the 1,500 men of the fighter group and its supporting units were still secure in their cots. Many others, though, had been awake all night as numerous shops and offices at the field required twenty-four-hour manning.

"Among those awake and, hopefully, alert were the CQs (Charge of Quarters), an old army term for the non-commissioned officers who man every unit's Orderly Room during off-duty hours. It is a job that rotates among all the unit's NCOs. With the coming of daylight, the three squadron CQs go forth from the Orderly Room to rouse the pilots and ground crews. They had been jarred from late night lethargy by a telephone call from Group Operations which, at some time during the night, had received by teletype machine, the Field Order for the coming mission from 66th Fighter Wing.

"The Field Order originating from Eighth Air Force Headquarters spells out the mission objectives, units involved, bomber routes to the target, fighter rendezvous times and locations, radio codes and all other information needed for the unit to play its part in the continuing air assault on Germany.

"As the CQ goes from hut to hut the routine is the same. He steps through the blackout door, flips on the light switch and says in a loud voice, 'Briefing 0700, maximum range, maximum effort.' Normally, only the wake-up time varies, depending on the pilot's briefing time. In the case of the pilots' barracks, he wakes only those scheduled to fly today.

"The first item on the agenda is breakfast at the big consolidated mess hall or the officers' mess. From there it is off to the flight line via GI truck, bicycle, or on foot, a distance of about one mile. With the crews on their way to the Mustangs huddled under their covers, and the pilots drifting into Group Briefing, the day's activities begin to accelerate.

"For centuries large military bases have tended to be self-contained cities. Leiston airfield, USAAF Station F-373, like dozens of other Eighth Air Force installations which sprawl across East Anglia, is no exception.

"The 1,500 men (and half a dozen women who run the Red Cross Club) provide all of the usual town services and a few others of a more warlike nature. The mission of these 1,500 men is to place a few to as many as sixty-five P-51 Mustang fighter planes and their pilots over Europe every day if ordered to do so, to enable them to take on the German military and win World War II. Everything on the station revolves around some ninety Mustangs and their pilots.

"The Yoxford Boys, the members of the USAAF's 357th Fighter Group, had been in residence at Leiston for about one year. Air operations are not really what we are talking about here. It is, however, worth noting that the 357th is among the highest-scoring fighter groups in the Eighth Air Force.

"January 1945 proved to be the coldest and one of the most difficult months for flying weather the group had experienced. For eighteen days of the month, the ground and runways had either been frozen or covered with snow and ice. On the fourteenth of that month, a date which has since become known as 'the big

day,' the group became engaged in a great air battle in the Berlin area and was credited with fifty-five and a half enemy fighters shot down, the highest one-day score ever among U.S. fighter groups.

"On this more typical day we have left the ground crews on their way to their individual aircraft. It was not always obvious to those outside of aviation—or to some in it—how critically important quality maintenance is in the operation of airplanes. In military operations it can mean the difference between success and failure of the mission, and the specter of aircraft and crew loss due to mechanical failure is always uppermost in the minds of the ground crews. Across the North Sea from Leiston, German air force commander Hermann Goering

said of his ground crews: 'Without their service, nothing can be achieved. I must say that their endurance, their skill, their patience, although different, is in every way the equal of that of the air crews.' Certainly, that praise applies equally to the ground crews of all the air forces in the war.

"In the 357th there were two levels of maintenance, the flight line crews assigned to individual aircraft, and the hangar crews which handled heavy maintenance such as engine changes. A third, higher level, on the Leiston base, the 469th Service Squadron, did the more complicated jobs that the squadrons were not equipped to do.

"When ground crews were mentioned, which was seldom, the reference was usually to the crew chiefs.

Most Eighth Air Force fighter units assigned three men to each airplane. Besides the crew chief (a sergeant or 'buck' sergeant). Those selected as crew chiefs were usually in their twenties—or the very elderly—in their thirties. Unless one is on 'other duty,' both the crew chief and assistant arrived at their aircraft at the same time.

"Their first duty was to remove the cockpit and wing covers and pitot tube cover. Then the propeller was pulled through its arc a few times and the pre-flight inspection started. The P-51 is remarkably simple. Nevertheless, the pre-flight, as laid out in the manual, is quite lengthy. Most of it consists of visual inspections, many of which had been completed during the post-flight inspection

the day before. All reservoirs were checked for fluid level, coolant, hydraulics, battery, engine oil, and fuel. An inspection was always made under the aircraft for coolant leaks, which frequently occurred due to temperature changes. It was often difficult to tell coolant from water, but touching a bit of the fluid with the tongue would reveal the difference, as coolant has a bitter taste (and is poisonous if consumed in quantity).

"If all visual and servicing checks are satisfactory, the engine run is done, using the battery cart to save the airplane's internal battery. Because the seat is rather deep (to accommodate the pilot's dinghy pack), a cushion in the seat helps one to reach the brakes and to see out from the cockpit. Now the brakes are set and

the seat belt fastened around the control stick to provide 'up elevators' during the power check. The flaps are left down, the fuel selector is set to either main tank, the throttle cracked open, and the mixture control set to the idle cut-off position. After yelling 'clear' to be sure no one is near the nose of the plane, the starter switch is engaged (the P-51 has a direct-drive starter), along with engine prime. As soon as the cylinders begin to fire, the mixture control is moved to 'run.' The propeller is already in full increase rpm for the warm-up. Various additional checks are now carried out, including checking that the engine oil and coolant temperature instruments are registering 'in the green.' The engine is run up to 2,300 rpm and the magnetos are checked. With each mag off,

the maximum allowable rpm drop is 100. The propeller governor is also checked at this rpm. The maximum rpm is 3,000, but this is for takeoff and is not used on the ground run.

"After the engine is shut down and everything has checked out OK, it is mostly a matter of waiting. The fuel and oil trucks cruise the taxiway and all tanks are topped off after the run. Now the windshield, canopy, and rear-view mirror are all polished—for the tenth time. The armament man has long since arrived and charged his guns, so all aircraft on the field have 'hot' guns long before takeoff. The gun switches in the cockpit were off, of course, but occasionally one had been left on and the pilot gripping the stick could fire a burst, terrifying everyone within range, including himself.

"The pilots usually arrived fifteen to twenty minutes before engine start time, via an overloaded jeep or weapons carrier. After the pilot was strapped in with the help of the ground crew, his goggles and windshield were given a final swipe. Engine start time came and sixty Merlins coughed into life around the airfield hardstands. Then the wheel chocks were pulled, and with a wave of his hand to the ground crew, each pilot guided his fighter out to the proper place on the taxi strip in a snake-like procession toward the active runway.

"The ground crews, and everyone else in the area, sought a vantage point to watch the takeoff—always an exciting event. The sight and sound of sixty or more overloaded Mustangs getting airborne was impressive.

"Much of the weight the planes are carrying is represented by two long-range fuel drop tanks, so vital to the success of the U.S. fighters in Europe. Most of these tanks are made of paper composition units (though some are metal), each holding 108 U.S. gallons, and were built in huge quantities by British companies. They were installed on the wing racks for the next day's mission the night before and filled at that time. During operation they were pressurized to ensure positive feeding at altitude, by the exhaust side of the engine vacuum pump. The piping for this and fuel flow was rubber tubes with glass elbows which would break away cleanly when the tanks were dropped. Even though the drop tanks were pressurized, it was necessary to coax

fuel into the system during the pre-flight. After switching to the 'drop tank' position the engine would often die, and the selector switch had to be quickly put back to 'main' and then to 'drop tanks' until they fed properly. On the mission they were always dropped when empty, or earlier if combat demanded it. With all fifteen fighter groups operating, Eighth Air Force fighters could require 1,800 drop tanks per day.

"At midday, while the mission aircraft were out, the line crews were in a state of suspended animation. It was mostly free time, time to attend to laundry, read the squadron bulletin board to see when mail call was, and to see if your name appeared on any unwanted, but unavoidable, extra duty rosters. There was also time to drop

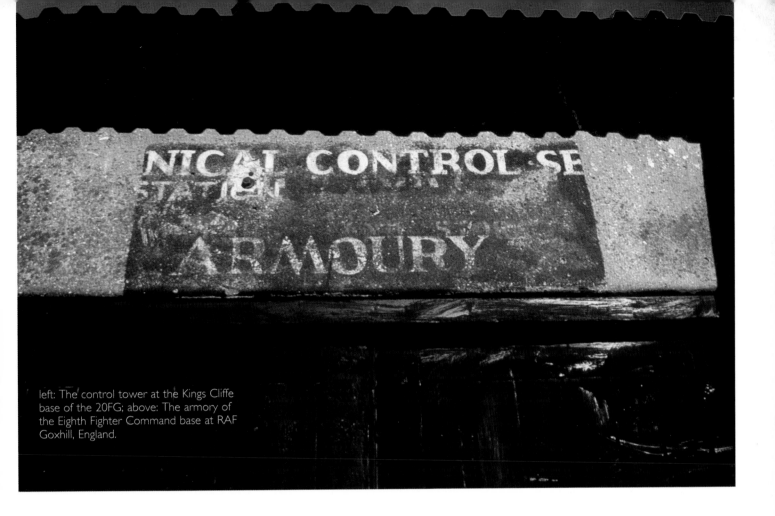

left: The control tower at the Kings Cliffe base of the 20FG; above: The armory of the Eighth Fighter Command base at RAF Goxhill, England.

into the Post Exchange for a candy bar, and to take in noon chow at the big consolidated mess hall.

"Regardless of what they have been doing while the mission was out, the aircraft ground crew always 'sweated out' the return of their particular airplane and pilot, and when both returned safely it was a great relief. Whether a crew had a close relationship with their pilot depended on several factors—how long they had been together, the pilot's general attitude towards enlisted men, and if he was an outgoing individual.

"Although the word 'hero' probably never occurred to the ground crews, they were well aware that it was their pilot who was doing the fighting, and sometimes the dying. In most cases, there was considerable affection for

their pilot and they were proud of his achievements. There was always a period of depression when an aircraft and pilot failed to return from a mission, and often the cause didn't filter down to the ground crew. In a day or two, a new P-51 arrived, and a new pilot, and the war went on.

"An average mission of the 357th Fighter Group lasted about four to five hours and by the ETR (estimated time of return) everyone was back on the hardstands. If the group came into sight in proper formation and to the rising snarl of many Merlins, it was probably that there had been no combat. If they straggled back in small groups, or individually, it was certain that there had been some kind of action. Missing red tape around the gun nozzles was a final confirmation.

"As each P-51 turned into its parking place, the pilot blasted the tail around and shut down the engine, the wheels were chocked, and the mission was over—one more toward completion of his tour. Now he brought any aircraft malfunctions to the attention of the crew, and departed for debriefing. For the ground crew there was considerable work ahead to complete the post-flight inspection and repair the aircraft. If luck was with them, their airplane could be 'put to bed' in time for evening chow, and the work day would have come to an end. Often though, it did not work out that way, and their jobs continued into the night.

"Our narrative started before dawn in a dreary January day. On another day that month, the 16th, two days after

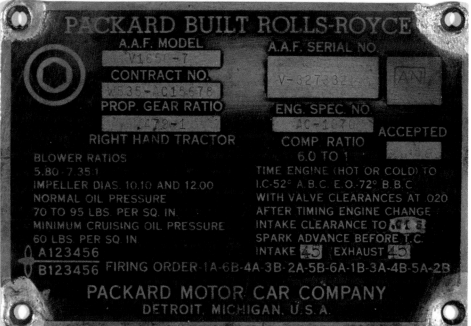

the group's astounding success over Berlin, Major Guernsey Carlisle led fifty-four Mustangs on a heavy bomber escort mission. He reported: 'Take-off 0924, down approx 1600 at various bases on continent. Group rendezvoused with bombers at 1100 Zwolle at 24,000. Left bombers at 1400 at Strasbourg. Weather bad. 10/10 cloud over target. Group instructed to land on continent, returned to UK on 19th January. Lieutenant William Thompson, 363rd, killed in crash near Framlingham.'

"Thompson was a victim of the bad weather, only a few miles from home base. He was one of seven who died during January. One of these was Staff Sergeant Melvin Schuneman, a crew chief and the only 357th ground crewman to die in an aircraft accident. He was killed on the 27th in another weather-related crash, along with pilot Lieutenant Walter Corby, in the group's AT-6.

"Leiston airfield was within a few miles of the North Sea coast and was often the first airfield seen by American and British pilots of battle-damaged aircraft returning from raids over the Continent. Many such cripples landed there with varying degrees of success. One of these incidents ended in a fiery spectacle in late May 1944 and is described here by Captain William O'Brien, USAF (Ret): 'After a mission flown in the early afternoon, I was in the cockpit of my plane, and my crew chief, Jim Loter, was standing on the wing. We saw a P-47 taxiing from south to north on the perimeter track on the 363rd side of the field. The Jug was moving fairly slowly, and he then pulled into an empty hardstand just across from where I was parked. As he turned, I could see white smoke starting to come from the lower fuselage, well back from the engine, about where

top left: A USAF fighter crew chief during the Gulf War; top right: Former 357FG Mustang crew chief Merle Olmsted; above: A Packard manufacturer's plate for a Merlin engine to power a North American Mustang fighter; right: Rearming a Debden-based P-51C of the 4FG, Eighth Air Force Fighter Command.

A cannon-armed Spitfire fighter on an RAF base in WWII.

the turbo supercharger was located. I told Jim to try and get to the Jug with our fire extinguisher as the pilot shut down the engine. The smoking aircraft was facing to the west, and about this time its guns started to fire and the pilot was out of the plane and standing on the hardstand. It is well known that the Jug had eight .50 caliber machine-guns. All eight were firing and believe me, that was the first and only time I'd ever heard that much firepower released. Needless to say, neither Loter or I could get to the Jug, which proceeded to burn and fire its guns. I imagine everyone within four miles wondered what the hell had happened.

"The story I got was, the Jug pilot was short on fuel—to the extent that he might not make it, and landed at the first base he saw, planning to refuel and then proceed to home base. He got refueled all right and was taxiing to take off when he heard a loud bang, so he pulled into the nearest hardstand. He had been doing some strafing on the way home from his mission. The "loud bang" was probably a 20mm or larger shell that had been lodged in the fuselage and finally exploded, possibly caused by taxiing across a rough spot, which was enough to activate the fuse. This jug pilot was one lucky man!'

"Gunfire of a more serious nature hit Leiston airfield two weeks later. Compared with the experience of the RAF during the Battle of Britain, and the German ground crews in 1944–45, life on an Eighth Air Force base was a relatively safe existence. Our pilots, the only ones on station doing the fighting, faced death or capture every day, but only once in the fourteen months of wartime service did Leiston airfield encounter hostile gunfire.

"On the night of D-Day, June 6–7, 1944, the Luftwaffe struck back at the Allies in retaliation for the invasion. According to RAF records, several bombs fell on Tuddenham, and five bombs were dropped in the vicinity of Parham and Framlingham, both only a few miles from Leiston. Three night-flying B-24s were attacked and one was shot down just after midnight. An RAF 25 Squadron Mosquito encountered and shot down an Me 410 forty miles east of Southwold.

"Shortly after midnight a German intruder struck at Leiston airfield. The field, like all of England then, was blacked out, but apparently the door to the mess hall, then serving midnight chow, had been left open. Attracted by this light the intruder fired a burst of cannon fire into the building, doing little damage other than making a few holes.

"Among those present there has always been much confusion and disagreement about the details of the event. The type of German aircraft has never been authenticated. Group records indicate it was probably an Me 410, but two men who were outside and got a close look at it say that it was a single-engine type, an Me 109 or Fw 190. Since neither of these types was really suitable for night raids on England, it was probably an Me 410, possibly the same one shot down by the Mosquito.

"Sergeant James Frary made a detailed entry about the incident in his diary: 'I was standing outside the Orderly Room (I was CQ that night) and there was a red alert on at the time. I heard the plane coming in low from the south. I didn't think about it being German until he reached the edge of the field and I could see him silhouetted against the sky. Just as a precaution I crouched down in front of the door. About then our AA guns started to fire. Pink tracers were going all around the enemy ship. Just as he

got almost out of my range of vision he banked around to the east and cut across the communal site. It was then that he cut loose with his guns, putting three holes in the mess hall and plowing up the baseball field with his 20mm guns. The AA fired about 300 rounds of caliber .50 and eight rounds of 40mm at him as he crossed the field. They apparently hit him as a gas cap and some scraps of metal were found later.

"Out on the flight line, Claude Allen of the 363rd Squadron remembered: 'It was about midnight and I had just been to the mess hall, and then to our squadron area to pick up the mail and some blankets as several of us from A Flight usually slept out on the line near the ships. I was driving the bomb service truck and a Sergeant Van Tyne was riding with me. While returning to the flight line we stopped at the radio shack just off the perimeter track and were informed that an alert had been in affect, but as all seemed clear, I pulled back on the perimeter track toward A Flight area. Suddenly we heard this loud drone overhead which sounded like an aircraft making a sharp turn, coming in from the direction of Leiston, and we could see the flash from the aircraft's guns. This is when I went out of the left side of the truck, my partner out the right side. About the time we were flat on the ground, the ack-ack opened up. When it was over we found the truck which had gone only a short distance before stopping, but did not see any damage to it.'

"The fourteen months on Eighth Fighter Command's Leiston airfield was a unique experience for the ground crews, and probably the high point of life for many. Most of us, however, did not appreciate this at the time, and wanted only to get it

over with and go home. Only in later years did some realize what a fascinating time it had been, and many of us have returned several times to the now tranquil land that once housed a fighter group at war."

Stretched out in the shade on the grass, / Talking with others who'd gathered around, / Crew chiefs were waiting for time to pass / Until their planes were back on the ground. / All night long some of them had worked, / Making their birds ready to go; / They knew o'er enemy skies what lurked . . . / And so the tension began to grow. / Five hours now and no sign / Of their fighters in friendly skies; Each was dying to shout: "There's mine!" / There were only nervous glances and sighs. / Then a speck was spotted far off, / Joined by others as they streaked down; / They swooped low and an engine did cough . . . / That crew chief wore a worried frown. / A six-hour mission, they peeled up to land / And all came back except for one lad; / His mechanic friend tried to understand . . . / Slowly he walked away, tearful and sad.
—*One Is Missing* by Bert McDowell, Jr.

I am grateful to my friend Merle Olmsted for generously sharing his memories of life on Leiston airfield in World War II. —*author*

An RAF Tornado in a Quick Reaction Alert shelter at the Leuchars base in Scotland.

I know that I shall meet my fate /
Somewhere among the clouds above;
/ Those that I fight I do not hate, /
Those that I guard I do not love. / My
country is Kiltartan Cross, / My coun-
trymen Kiltartan's poor. / No likely
end could bring them loss / Or leave
them happier than before. / Nor law
nor duty bade me fight, / Nor public
men nor cheering crowds, / A lonely
impulse of delight / Drove to this
tumult in the clouds; / I balanced all,
brought all to mind, / The years to
come seemed waste of breath / A
waste of breath the years behind / In
balance with this life, this death.
—*An Irish Airman Foresees His Death*
by William Butler Yeats

"It isn't always being fast or accurate
that counts, it's being willing. I found
out early that most men, regardless
of cause or need, aren't willing. They
blink an eye or draw a breath before
they pull a trigger. I won't."
—John Bernard Books, title character
in *The Shootist*

"WHEN YOU'VE GOT A GOOD HOLD on
the enemy's tail and are clobbering
him well, it seems then he never will
die. Each part of a second doesn't
feel like time at all, but is slow, so
very slow and so endless. Armor-
piercing incendiaries hit him all over.
They cloud him up all over and
go all over him like snake tongues.
That's what they look like—little red
snake tongues, hundreds of them,
flicking him poisonously all over.
That goes on and on, each little flick
quick as a twist, but the whole thing
so slow, so endless.

"Then black smoke starts out of
him and goes slowly and endlessly
out of him. At first it comes as if
you've squeezed it out of him and
then a cloud of it appears. Glycol is
the fluid that keeps the motor from

overheating. You can't fly more than
a minute or so without it. It comes
out into the air looking white, and
when you see it coming out well, in a
pour, then that's the end.

"The wind of death blowing up to
storm proportions in him. It's a small
pour at first, usually thin, like a frosty
breath, then bigger, bigger, bigger and
always slow and endless and stuck
into your eyes and stopped there like
a movie held still.

"And after that, sometimes when
you're really clobbering him and are
really all over him, hammering his guts
out, pieces start coming off him. It's
nuts-and-bolts stuff at first, then bigger
things, big, ripped-off-looking things
as if you're tearing arms and legs off
him and arms and legs and the head
of him are going slowly, endlessly over
your shoulder."
—Major Don Gentile, formerly with
the 4th Fighter Group, Eighth USAAF

Thomas J. Moore flew Mustangs with
the 361st Fighter Group at Bottisham,
Cambridgeshire, and at Little Walden,
Essex, in England: "I do not think
being a shooter is the fighter pilot's
most important asset. I think the more
important aspect would be the ability
to get into position behind the enemy
or even for a deflection shot; this
would enhance a chance for victory. A
pilot might miss on a deflection shot
but still might be able to get behind
the enemy, or get a more accurate
small angle shot."

"I started flying the American Curtiss
P-36 with 1/5 *Groupe de Chasse* of
the French Air Force. The P-36 handled very well and was armed and
better than any of the French aircraft
of that time.

"On May 12th, 1940 over the
town of Sedan, I saw that a bunch of
Ju 87 Stukas were dive-bombing the

357FG pilot John England, in cockpit
of his Mustang *Nooky Booky IV* on the
group's Leiston base, having just returned
from a bomber escort mission.

town. I didn't even notice that they were protected by some Me 109s as I positioned myself behind one of the Stukas. He went down from only two short bursts of my gun. In four minutes I brought down four Ju 87s, using less than 250 shells altogether. I did not open fire until I was less than 100 yards behind the German planes. One Me 109 fired at my plane, but it didn't seem to be badly damaged and I flew back to our airfield. On landing, a German bullet was found that had passed through my fuselage and stopped in the protective steel plate by where my neck had been. Only then did I realize how close I was to my death, and my knees turned to jelly."

—Generalmajor Frantisek Perina, formerly of No 312 (Czech) Squadron, RAF

"We were not, thank God, involved in the intimate, personal killing of men which is the lot of the infantry—though we fired with the same bloody end in view. The men inside the aircraft must be killed or maimed or taken prisoner, otherwise they would return to battle. Very few of us thought of it that way, and this gave to our battle in the air the character of a terribly dangerous sport and not of a dismal, sordid slaughter."

—Group Captain Peter Townsend, No 85 Squadron RAF.

Group Captain Al Deere, formerly with No 54 Squadron, RAF: "Personally, I was never a good shot. I know from my work with a shotgun, I was an average shot, whereas Colin Gray, my fellow New Zealander in 54 Squadron, was above average, so it was easier for him than for me. Each chap worked out his own tactics. I soon worked it out, but I had to get bloody close, otherwise I wouldn't have got the guy

down. The range was supposed to be at 400 yards, which was ridiculous. You had to be able to shoot, but you didn't have to be an exceptional shot. It's no good shooting well if you can't fly the aircraft well. So, if you could fly the aircraft well you could, to a degree, overcome your lack of ability in natural shooting. The best shots in the [Royal] Air Force were chaps who could shoot birds on the wing with a shotgun. I could, but not to their extent. The best shot in the Air Force, I think, was 'Sailor' Malan. He was a contemporary of mine at Hornchurch."

Colonel John W. Cunnick, USAF (Ret), formerly with the 55th Fighter Group, Eighth USAAF: "In our day, fighter pilots spent many hours shooting skeet and trap to learn about leading and lagging our targets. However, after reviewing hundreds of kills on gun camera film, I believe that more than 90 percent of them were made from dead astern. Every fifth round in our ammo belts was an incendiary tracer. Their primary use was to ignite fires; the secondary use was to give us a look at where our ammo was going. In fact, the incendiary trajectory wasn't the same as our standard rounds."

Feldwebel Oscar Boesch, formerly with *Sturm Staffel 1*, IV/JG3 "Udet"': "To be a good shot was essential. Every dogfight is a duel, and deadly."

Captain Harvey Mace, USAF (Ret), formerly with the 357th Fighter Group, Eighth USAAF: "Marksmanship was important, but most kills were made by virtually poking the gun barrels up their butts."

"What counts is not necessarily the size of the dog in the fight—it's the size of the fight in the dog."

—General (later President) Dwight D. Eisenhower, 1958

Kazimierz Budzik flew Spitfires with No 308 (Polish) Squadron RAF. His combat record includes two operational tours and a score of kills and probables. But he dismissed any suggestion of heroism. "Heroes? I don't know what they are. There were many brave deeds done, of course. Mostly, though, heroes were born out of spur-of-the-moment actions. Most of the time, like everyone else, I was just concerned with self-preservation."

Colonel Walker M. Mahurin, USAF (Ret), formerly with the 56th Fighter Group, Eight USAAF, came from Fort Wayne, Indiana. One of his mathematics teachers once wrote to him: "I never was impressed with your ability to solve algebra or geometry problems. The fact is, I didn't think you'd ever amount to a damn."

In World War II, Mahurin spent most of his combat career with the 56th, "Zemke's Wolf Pack." It is probably fair to say that Hub Zemke and Bud Mahurin were something less than close friends. Mahurin found himself in trouble with his commanding officer on several occasions. Bud was naturally aggressive and was never shy about showing initiative in the group. While he was flying missions from Halesworth in his P-47 Thunderbolt, it was VIII Fighter Command policy that its fighters, when assigned to escort the B-17s and B-24s of Eighth Bomber Command, were to stay with the bombers—period. On a number of missions, however, Mahurin decided that if he saw a German fighter, he was going to go get it. "The first two that I got were some distance from us, queuing up to go into the bomber stream. Later, Hub was going to court-martial me for leaving the

Colonel Francis Gabreski was the highest-scoring American fighter ace of WWII in Europe, credited with 34 1/2 enemy aircraft destroyed in the air , including 6 1/2 in the Korean War.

bomber stream. When he went down to see General Kepner about charging me, the general said: 'Well, you go ahead if you feel you want to, but in the meantime I'm gonna give him a Silver Star.'

"The excitement and the thrill associated with shooting down an enemy airplane is indescribable. I always liken it to a big-game hunt, only here the quarry had the same advantage as you. Boy, it's touch-and-go, but Jesus, is it thrilling. I think the most fun and most excitement I

ever had was flying an F-86 in Korea against the Russians. That was just sheer delight and pleasure.

"In Europe though, we were bore-sighted for 300 yards, and at that range the pattern would be a square of about twelve feet. The natural tendency was to fire way out of range. With the first two airplanes I got, I came home with German oil on my airplane and on the windshield. But lots of times I fired out of range. Lots of times I took 'snap-shots' and didn't have the presence of mind

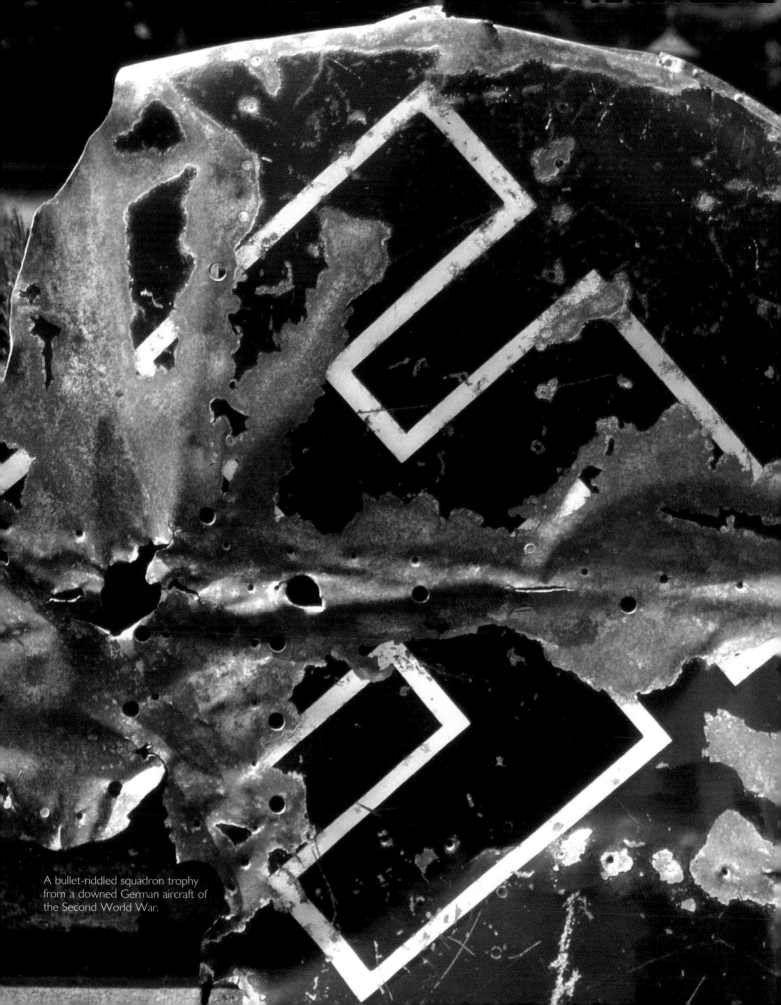

A bullet-riddled squadron trophy from a downed German aircraft of the Second World War.

to slow down and take things easy and really get lined up. But the more experienced one became, the closer one got to the enemy airplane, and as more inexperienced German pilots were encountered, the easier it was.

"But the perspective—we just didn't have training aids that were good enough to simulate ranges as the range would look in the gunsight—to show, for example, what a 109 would look like out there at 600 yards, so you could get a perspective. In theory, we were supposed to be able to control the circle so you could set it for the wingspan of, say, a Focke-Wulf Fw 190, and if the airplane filled the circle, you were within range. Except, how the hell are you gonna do that when it went this way and that way and up and down and sideways? You just couldn't do it.

"I was in several dogfights. With the Me 110s, most of my kills were rear-quartering stern shots; most were real stern chases where they were wide open, and they knew we were behind them and we were closing very slowly. If you couldn't get into that kind of position, your chances of hitting the guy would be a question of how good you were at aerial combat, and most of us weren't that good.

"I've been on any number of missions where there was fighting going on all over the sky and I couldn't find out where the hell they were. Bob Johnson, or Gabreski . . . I'd hear those guys shooting, but it was happening in a different part of the sky, and by the time I got over there, there wasn't any more fight because it had happened so fast. You had to be in the right place at the right time.

"One of the advantages that Hub Zemke and the 56th Fighter Group had was that we were one of the three senior groups in England and we got the P-47s first and had had them

in the United States beforehand. We were allowed to escort the lead box of the bombers, so we were up in front, and the Germans were gonna attack the lead box. We had more exposure than the other wings did, and that was very, very important, as far as victories went."

"Fighter pilots have to be good shooters, by born ability or by increasing experience. But certainly, we couldn't select pilots according to those qualities as we were short on fighter pilots."
—Generalleutnant a.D. Günther Rall, German air force (Ret)

"Being a great shooter . . . important, yes! Most important, no. Give a poor marksman a good shot and he will get you."
—Captain William O'Brien, USAF (Ret), formerly with the 357th Fighter Group, Eighth USAAF

"With the exception of Albert Ball, most crack fighters did not get their Huns in dogfights. They preferred safer means. They would spend hours synchronizing their guns and telescopic sights so that they could do accurate shooting at, say, 200 or 300 yards. They would then set out on patrol, alone, spot their quarry (in such cases usually a two-seater doing reconnaissance or photography), and carefully maneuver for position, taking great pains to remain where they could not be seen, i.e. below and behind the tail of the enemy. From here, even if the Hun observer did spot them, he could not bring his gun to bear without the risk of shooting away his own tail plane or rudder. The stalker would not hurry after his quarry, but keep a wary eye to see he was not about to be attacked himself. He would gradually draw nearer, always in the blind spot, sight his

guns very carefully, and then one long deadly burst would do the trick.

"Such tactics as those were employed by Captain McCudden, VC, DSO, and also by Guynemeyer, the French ace. Both of them, of course, were superb if they got into a dogfight; but it was in such fighting that they were both ultimately killed."
—from *Sagittarius Rising* by Cecil Lewis, No 56 Squadron, RFC

U.S. Marine Corps pilot John Bolt was a member of Marine VMF-214, Gregory Boyington's "Black Sheep Squadron" from June 1943. Jack Bolt flew the F4U Corsair with 214. In the Korean War he flew F9F-4 Panthers, and F-86 Sabres on an exchange tour with the U.S. Air Force. He remains the only jet ace in Marine Corps aviation history and the only man in U.S. Navy aviation history to become an ace in two wars: "It takes a while to develop real expertise in a combat situation. You're not very effective on your first few contacts with the enemy. I estimate that I have been in fifty firing contacts with enemy fighters—with either me shooting at them or them shooting at us—in World War II and the Korean War. After you've been in ten to fifteen contacts, you're a different person. The ones who are most frightened are the ones most at risk. I was certainly a slow learner.

"Most kills were made by sneaking up on a guy. He would be preoccupied with what was going on all around him, and he would not be watching the very narrow cone through his tail from which he was most vulnerable. If we had a good speed advantage, we would try to get down low as we came in behind him because he could not see there. It was more difficult for him to see us than when we were higher up. If we got within firing range, we closed in to tail him until we were ready to fire, and being fifty or a hundred feet below him put us in his blind area. If he knew we were coming, he was really hard to kill. There was just that narrow little shooting position, in behind him, from which he was going to get killed."

"Whatever may have been previously written, it is fact that fighter pilots never found deflection shooting easy, for a variety of reasons. Some of the 'aces' were better at it than the majority, but in the main, the enemy were shot down by attacking fighters 300 yards astern and a three-second burst of machine-gun fire right up the arse."
—Pilot Officer Nick Berryman, RAF (Ret), formerly with No 276 Squadron

Lieutenant Commander H. B. Moranville, US Navy (Ret): "On December 14, 1944, while assigned to VF-11, the Sun Downers, and flying an F6F-5 Hellcat from the aircraft carrier *Hornet* (CV-12), I was approaching the island of Luzon in the Philippines when we spotted a very large Japanese transport escorted by a destroyer and a destroyer escort. My division leader, Jim Swope, immediately signaled that we would make a run on the transport. We were all equipped with the normal six .50 caliber guns plus, on this flight, we had six five-inch armor-piercing rockets under our wings. The usual procedure for rocket attacks was to divide the division into two two-plane sections and make a co-ordinated attack from different directions, and that's what we proceeded to do. As usual you could not observe whether you had hit the target with your rockets, but as you retired from the attack you could observe whether you had caused any damage. It appeared that

we had numerous hits and there were several fires on the ship.

"As I was recovering from the rocket run, my aircraft was hit by three 20mm or 40mm antiaircraft projectiles. I was immediately aware that I had been hit, but it did not appear that my Hellcat had been damaged too much. When the division joined up after the rocket run, my wingman, Ensign Eddie Kearns, and Lieutenant Jim Swope both looked me over and, although they spotted some holes in the fuselage, it didn't look like there was much serious damage, and I decided to continue on the strike. One thing bothered me more than a little, though. The red 'beer-can'-shaped WING LOCKED indicators (one in each wing) were both showing that my wings were unlocked. After the first panicky feeling, I figured out that just the cable that held the indicators down was cut, and that, since the actual locking pins were held in place by hydraulic pressure, there was no problem. In a few minutes, however, I noticed hydraulic fluid pouring over my starboard wing, and another moment of panic struck. Again, I analyzed the situation and figured that the pins would require actual hydraulic pressure to unlock them and, as I didn't have any hydraulic pressure, I didn't have to worry.

"Our secondary mission on this flight was to seek and destroy any airborne enemy aircraft that we found between Manila and Subic Bay. We flew down the Bataan Peninsula and did not spot any aircraft, and were returning to attack the transport by strafing.

"Just as we were leaving the Subic Bay area, I spotted a twin-engined Dinah aircraft and 'tallyhoed' it. In accordance with our division policy, I took the lead since I knew where the enemy plane was. I was in an excel-

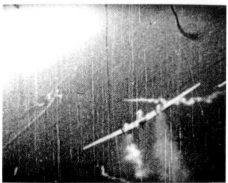

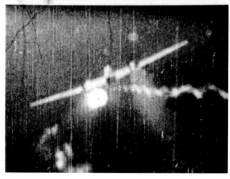

Allied gun camera sequence showing the downing of a German bomber early in the Second World War.

lent position to make a stern run on the Dinah and, since the enemy pilot took no evasive action, that's what I did. As there was no reason to hurry the attack, I waited until I was very close and, after a short burst from my guns, the starboard engine flamed and, almost immediately, the plane exploded and went down.

"Following the attack, we rejoined on Jim Swope and proceeded to Manila, where we found the Japanese transport dead in the water, and other carrier aircraft attacking the other ships in the convoy. We all joined in and made strafing runs on the destroyer. After a couple of runs it was time for the strike to be over so we headed back to the Task Force.

"When we arrived over the *Hornet*, we made a break and went into a normal landing pattern. The first problem that occurred was when Jim Swope put his landing gear down. One gear went down and the other would not go anywhere but to the trail position. Next, my landing flaps would not go down. It took a few minutes to sort it out with the ship and, as I had a lot more fuel left than Swope, it was decided that he would land first. Everyone else in the recovery had landed by the time Jim went aboard. He made a good approach and landing. The crash crew quickly got his aircraft out of the arresting area, and it was my turn to land. It would be my first carrier landing with no flaps, but I felt it would be no problem. I made a good approach and got a 'Cut' from the landing signalman. I felt the hook engage a wire and, for an instant, felt relieved. But almost as soon as I felt the arrest, the plane began to accelerate again. My first thought was that I was going to flip over the side of the ship, but then I hit the first barrier and the prop wound up in the cables. The aircraft

tried to go over on its back, but when the prop spinner hit the deck it stopped. The deck crew immediately climbed up on the plane, helped me unhook all my equipment, and assisted me out of the cockpit. Fortunately, I was unhurt and I went on down to the Ready Room for a debriefing.

"Shortly after I entered the Ready Room, a flight deck crewman came to the door and asked for the pilot of the Hellcat that had just crashed. He came in and handed me the point of the arresting hook from my plane. When I landed without flaps, I was going a bit fast and the hook actually broke. He found the piece on the flight deck and thought I might like it as a souvenir. How right he was."

Ivan Kojedub, Russia's highest-scoring ace of World War II, came from a poor peasant family in the Ukraine. He struggled in his studies but finally was accepted into a technical college and joined a state-sponsored flying club there. Early in 1940, he earned a pilot's license and was accepted for flying training in the Red Air Force. He progressed quickly and, at an Operational Conversion Unit near Moscow, was introduced to the new Lavochkin La-5 radial-engined fighter which he was to fly with amazing success against the best machine of the Luftwaffe, the Focke-Wulf Fw 190.

"In the wings of our planes was mounted a 16mm movie camera, which started taking pictures as soon as the guns were fired. If no other pilots could verify your claim, the films would bear witness to your marksmanship. The films were rushed to Eighth Air Force Headquarters, where assessments were made; one was spliced together with an appropriate heading giving the pilot's name and claim, along with other movies taken

from other pilots of the same date, and this was shown on the next day to the group. A movie room had been set up in the back of the photo lab so that pilots could observe the previous day's shooting. I couldn't wait this long. That night I went to the photo officer's room to ask about my film. Did it show any strikes? His answer discouraged me. 'Not a thing, Johnny. There wasn't even a picture of a German plane on the film.' "
—from *The Look of Eagles* by Major John T. Godfrey

Colonel Gidi Livni flew F-16s in the Israeli Air Force for fourteen years: "Great gunnery is a key factor in scoring fast kills while saving ammunition. The good shooter is able to snap-shot the enemy while he crosses the gunsight line.

"During the Yom Kippur War [1973] two of my kills were achieved through snap-shooting at close range, low speed and a high-aspect angle.

"Gunnery today is much easier. All-aspect missiles can be launched at any angle. The missile 'eye' is slaved to various sensor sources such as radar, a helmet sight, etc. and the shooting envelope is calculated by computers. Nowadays, pilots are expected to be highly skilled and sensitive in order to operate the various switches and buttons on the stick and the throttle . . . switches that slave, release, lock or designate the radar and missile 'eyes,' select weapon modes, and activate self-defense devices."

"The whole thing goes in a series of whooshes. There is no time to think. If you take time to think you will not have time to act. There are a number of things your mind is doing while you are fighting—seeing, measuring, guessing, remembering, adding up this and that and worrying about one thing

Mustangs of the 357FG over England in 1944.

and another, and taking this into account and that into account and rejecting this notion and accepting that notion. But it doesn't feel like thinking.

"After the fight is over you can look back on all the things you did and didn't do and see the reason behind each move. But while the fight is on, your mind feels empty and feels as if the flesh of it is sitting in your head, bunched up like muscle and quivering there."
—Major Don Gentile, formerly with the 4th Fighter Group, Eighth USAAF

Commander Randy Cunningham, US Navy (Ret), flew F-4 Phantoms from the carrier *Constellation* during

the Vietnam War. May 10, 1972: "With the beginning of Operation Linebacker [a new and relatively unrestricted bombing offensive authorized by President Nixon against North Vietnam], and now the mining [of Haiphong harbor to deny it to Russian ships], apprehension dominated my thoughts. I suppose all fighter pilots like to think of themselves as indestructable, unbeatable, fearless . . . but my mind would wander back to home, my wife and child and the possibility that I might not see them again. I often fought back tears and a lump in my throat. This brooding had come over me the morning of the 10th, only more consuming. A few days earlier I had received a 'Dear

John' letter from my wife. She wanted out of the marriage. The strain was almost unbearable. Just when I was feeling sorriest for myself, a voice bounced in 'Hey, Duke! What you doin', eatin' more bullets?'

"Flying with backseater Commander Willie 'Irish' Driscoll, we were close enough to count on each other in times of trouble, though we had our arguments, both in and out of the cockpit. The moment of brooding introspection was gone. As time went on our friendship grew stronger, and later I was to find Willie a major support in keeping me up when personal problems became almost unbearable. The Irishman was always there.

"The target was the Haiphong rail

yard that served as a funneling point for the Ban Kori, Mugia, and Napi mountain passes leading to the Ho Chi Minh Trail. It was smack in the middle of several MiG fields—Phuc Yen, Kep and Yen Bai on the way in; Dong Suong, Bai Thuong, Thanh Hoa, and Vinh on the way out. And the target itself was supposed to be heavily fortified with AAA ranging from 23mm to 120mm, not to mention SAMs along the flight path.

"The skipper looked over and smiled as he added our names to the strike roster as flak suppressors. Even though we'd be loaded with Rockeye bombs and would stay with the slower attack birds, once the bombs were away we still had four Sidewinder and two Sparrow stingers if the MiGs should want to play. It seemed so important for us to go, but then there were mixed feelings when our names were added, 'Maybe it's not such a good idea at that.' That old mixture of apprehension and aggressiveness.

"All strapped in, we waited for the 'start engines' call in the 100 percent humidity. Word filtered down the line there might be a cancellation due to bad weather, making me fume, but the order soon came that the mission was a go.

"Turbines whined as they picked up speed and aircraft were rolling up to the cat. Jet blast deflectors went up and the first aircraft was off. One by one, each took his turn on the four catapults until it was our turn. Hooked on to the cat, we ran up to 100 percent power, checked the instruments, lit the burners, saluted the cat officer, and WHAM . . . we were on our way, doing nearly 200 knots in just a few hundred feet.

"Brian and I were stepped up above the main strike force of A-6s and A-7s. Irish commented on what a shame such a beautiful country had to be bombed—winding waterways glistened through emerald-green valleys as the sun reflected off the roofs of the populated wetlands.

"The first attack had demolished the primary target, so CAG directed the remainder of the strike force to secondary targets. Brian and I were sent to the large supply area adjacent to the rail yard. We decided to close in tight to fighting wing formation and release simultaneously. We rolled over just as two SAMs were launched at us; failing to track, they came whizzing up past us. I looked back down at the target in time to see it disappear in a cloud of smoke and debris—A-7 1,000-pounders had leveled it flat.

"We rolled over a bit more and I picked up a long, red-brick storage building. Dropping our bombs, we pulled off the target and I made the mistake of looking back over my right shoulder to see what we had done to the target. My head was down and locked when Brian, being the superb wingman he was, called, 'Duke, you have MiG-17s at your seven o'clock, shooting!'

"Two 17s flew right by Brian's F-4, about 500 feet in front. I popped my wing back down and reversed hard port in time to see a 17 pull in behind and start firing.

"My first instinct was to break into him. Then I thought, 'I did that two days ago and the guy rendezvoused on me.' A quick glance at the MiG told me it was closing on me at high speed, meaning controls that were hard to move. I broke into him anyway.

"The MiG driver just didn't have the muscle to move that stick. He overshot the top of my two o'clock, but his wingman, who was back about 1,500 feet, pitched up and did a vertical displacement roll out to my belly side. 'Duke,' Brian called, 'I'll take care

of the guy at your six.' With utter confidence in Brian, I turned my attention back to the other MiG. When I squeezed off a Sidewinder, the enemy fighter was well within minimum range, but by the time the missile got to him he was about 2,500 feet out in front of me . . . that's how fast he was going. The 'Winder' blew him to pieces. That engagement lasted about fifteen seconds."

In the next few moments, Commander Cunningham and Commander Driscoll engaged and destroyed two additional enemy aircraft, including that of the North Vietnamese Air Force pilot known as "Colonel Tomb," who is believed to have had thirteen American aircraft to his credit.

Cunningham: "I pitched off, broke and headed out again in burner. As we neared Nam Dinh I heard another SAM call. Glancing over to starboard I watched an SA-2 heading straight for us. Before I could maneuver, the SAM went off. The resultant concussion was not too violent, but my head felt like it went down to my stomach. We had had closer SAM explosions than that and there appeared to be no damage. I immediately went to the gauges to check for systems malfunctions. Everything indicated normal so I continued to climb, watching for more SAMs. Irish couldn't understand how the thing got so close without our ECM gear's warning us. Neither could I.

"About forty-five seconds later the aircraft yawed violently to the left. 'What's the matter, Duke? You flying instruments again?' asked Irish. I steadied up and looked into the cockpit to see the PC-1 hydraulic system indicating zero, the PC-2 and utility systems fluctuating. Fear, that ever-present companion, wanted to run the ship. 'What now, Cunningham?' raced through my mind.

"Thank God for sea stories, for somewhere out of my memory bank came the recollection that 'Duke' Hernandez, another Navy pilot, had rolled his aircraft to safety after losing his hydraulics. When an F-4 loses hydraulics the stabilator locks, forcing the aircraft's nose to pitch straight up. The stick has no effect on the controls, only rudder and power are available when this happens.

"Sure enough, when PC-2 went to zero, the nose went straight up! I pushed full right rudder, yawing the nose to the right and forcing the nose down. As the nose passed through the horizon I selected 'idle' on the throttle and put out the speed brakes to prevent a power dive.

"I quickly transferred to left rudder, yawing the nose through the downswing to force it above the horizon. Full afterburner, retract speed brakes and the F-4 was in a climbing half roll. Just before the plane stalled at the top, the process was repeated.

"I rolled the Phantom twenty miles in this manner—I have no idea how many times, since all I cared about was making it to the water—beginning at 27,000 feet and working down to 17,000 by the time we reached the Red River Valley with wall-to-wall villages. The most fear I've ever known in my life was thinking that Irish and I were going to become POWs, especially if the enemy captors knew we had become the first American aces of the Vietnam War.

"The aircraft was burning just aft of Irish—I told him to reselect the ejection sequence handle so that if he decided to go, I wouldn't go with him. He asked why. I told him I wasn't about to spend nine or ten years in the Hanoi Hilton. 'Okay, Duke,' he replied. 'I'm staying with you until you give the word, but I'm placing the han-

dle so that we both go when I eject.'

"The next few seconds were full of fear—I even prayed, asking God to get me out of this. The aircraft rolled out, and I thought He didn't have anything to do with it. The the F-4 rolled uncontrollably again, and I thought to myself, 'God, I didn't mean it!'

"An explosion ripped through the Phantom and I almost ejected, but we were still over land. The radio was full of screams from our buddies to punch out. They knew the burning F-4 could explode any second. A-7s and F-4s were all around us—I caught glimpses of them as we rolled up and down. Any MiG wandering within ten miles of the area would have been sorry; a situation like this gets pilots hopping mad.

"Just as we crossed the coast we lost our last utility system and another violent explosion shook our fighter. A few seconds earlier and we would have been forced to come down in enemy territory. Someone up there must have heard my prayer. At that moment I prayed the classic 'foxhole' prayer and pledged to myself that I would seek to understand and accept Jesus if I made it.

"With the hydraulics gone, the rudder was useless. On the upswing I was unable to force the nose back down. The F-4 stalled and went into a spin.

"Each revolution I could see land, then ocean; incredible as it may seem, my fear kept me in the aircraft. I thought we were too close to the beach, and the winds normally blew landward. I told Irish to stay with me for two more turns a I attempted to break the spin and get some more water behind us. I deployed the drag chute with no effect—the controls were limp.

"Willie and I had often discussed what we would do should the need ever arise to leave our aircraft. I

would say, 'Irish, eject, eject, eject,' and he would pull the cord on the third 'eject.'

"'We are going to have to get out,' finally left my mouth.

"'Duke, the handle is set . . . when I go, you're going with me. Good luck!'

"I got out, 'Irish, e- . . .' and I heard his seat fire. There is only a split-second delay between the rear and front seats firing—if the front went out first, the rocket motor would fry the guy in back—but I heard his canopy go and thought my seat had malfunctioned. As I started to reach for the ejection cord, my seat fired, driving me up the rail and away from Showtime 100.

"There was no pain from the G-loading, then everything became quiet as I tumbled through space. I caught a glimpse of Willie's chute opening and, again, felt fear over the fact that something was not going to work and that I would not separate from my seat. But everything worked as advertised and I sailed away from the bulky seat.

"The chute lines rushed past me—I must have been going down head-first—then the chute opened with a crack-the-whip jolt. Sharp pain ran through my back.

"Beautiful, a full canopy, but the first thing I looked for was land—was I drifting towards it? The choking fear of capture grabbed me again as I saw enemy patrol boats, a large freighter and some junks coming out of the Red River towards us. I just knew I had no taste for pumpkin soup.

"Totally fixated on the boats, I was startled by the intrusion of Corsairs and Phantoms rolling in on the enemy vessels. Hey, they hadn't left us—and I knew they were low on fuel, yet they pressed through AAA and SAMs to turn the boats around. I felt small and alone floating down in my chute until my buddies made their presence

Walker "Bud" Mahurin was one of the greatest fighter pilots of WWII and the Korean War.

120 LONE EAGLE

known. I find it hard even now to express the gratitude that flooded my senses.

"Then it dawned on me that I had a survival radio! I could talk! 'May Day, May Day! This is Showtime. 100 Alpha is okay!' Willie was 100 Bravo.

"'Hang on, sailor. We're on our way,' replied the search and rescue team. Wow! In my joy I looked around for the first time. The biggest boost of the day was to see Irish a few hundred feet away waving like crazy to let me know he was okay. He flipped me the bird . . . no doubt about it, he was fine. I cordially returned the salute.

"We were really coming down slow, plenty of time to go through all the procedures we'd been taught, but never had to use until now. Then, for some unknown reason, my thoughts shifted to home and the 'Dear John' letter from my wife. I seriously questioned if I would have what it takes to go through the camps if I were captured. We had been told the two major sustaining forces in captivity would be a strong faith in God and a loving wife. I was deficient in both areas.

"Thinking about my wife, I cried like a baby for a minute or so. My life was falling apart in great emotional upheaval. Again, I vowed to change my life for the better if I got out of this.

"My mind jolted back to the present difficulties when the wind caught my survival raft, hanging several feet below me on a tether. I started to swing back and forth like a pendulum. At the top of each swing the side of my chute would tuck under and, having never parachuted before, I thought it would fold up and let me fall. The para-riggers later told me it was perfectly safe, but it served admirably in taking my mind off personal problems.

"About twenty feet above the water I jettisoned the parachute while looking down at my raft. I went belly-first into the warm, muddy water. Muddy? Struggling to the surface I found myself right in the mouth of the Red River. In scrambling for the tether attached to the raft I noticed something floating in the water next to me. A closer look revealed a rotting Vietnamese corpse, apparently washed down the river. For a second I thought it was Willie, but the body was too good-looking. I swam for my raft with Olympic speed.

"We were in the water fifteen minutes pending fifteen years, when three Marine helos from USS *Okinawa* hovered over. As fighter pilots we used to make jokes about those funny little machines with rotors that chugged along at just over 100 knots. My views changed radically at that moment.

"We were aboard in no time and on our way to the hospital ship. The president couldn't have been treated better. Everyone, from the ship's cook to the CO, came by to say hello and to ask if we needed anything. Doctors swarmed over us and we were checked for injuries. My back was stiff and out of place, but pronounced okay, so we boarded the helo again to get back to the *Connie*.

"As we circled CVA-64, we could see the decks lined with waving, cheering men. As we gently set down, the cheers were audible above the chopper's roar. My back was throbbing, but damned if I was going to be carried aboard on a stretcher. Irish helped me out of the chopper. By the time I had my feet on *Connie*'s deck the tears were flowing—Irish, too. It was impossible to express our joy at being home and not under a Vietcong gun."

left: Group Captain Adolph "Sailor" Malan came from South Africa to become one of the finest fighter leaders of the Battle of Britain. Fellow BofB ace Al Deere referred to Malan as the best shooter in the RAF; below: German ace Günther Rall; with 275 enemy aircraft downed, Rall was the third-highest-scoring fighter pilot in history.

Group Captain A. G. "Sailor" Malan was married and had a son during World War II. Prime Minister Winston Churchill stood as godfather to the boy. When sitting for his portrait by Captain Cuthbert Orde, Malan told the artist that having a wife and son had been of the greatest moral help to him during the Battle of Britain; that it gave him an absolutely definite thing to fight for and defend, and that this was his constant thought.

"Occasionally, we'd have a party at the base. The prerequisite for this was that there'd be a group of young ladies who'd be willing to come to the base for a dance or a party. These young ladies would come out and make themselves available and we would have a party at the officers' club. Usually, we'd stock up pretty good on hooch and food. The British had a tough, tough time feeding their population and these young ladies enjoyed the opportunity to have butter, white bread and roast beef. There was a lot of drinking and horsing around. Sometimes it took two or three days to get the base cleaned up and get the gals out."—a former Eighth USAAF officer

CAPTAIN GROVER C. HALL, JR. was public relations officer of the 4th Fighter Group at Debden, Essex, during World War II. His wartime diaries formed the basis of his book *1,000 Destroyed*, a history of the 4th in that war. In it, he referred to the group commanding officer, Colonel Don Blakeslee and his oft-quoted philosophy: "Fighter pilots and women don't mix." "He meant by that, that pilots had a way of getting cautious after Cupid bit. It was a fetching quote. The press services pounced on it while Blakeslee was on leave in New York. The quote became a box insert on the front pages of papers from coast to coast.

"Almost immediately Blakeslee was deluged with letters from all over the country from young ladies who had fighter pilots for husbands, fiancées or friends, and had always understood that they were, far from a combat opiate, the sustaining inspiration to the pilot in his mortal struggles with the Axis monsters. And now this iconoclastic, outrageous 'fighter pilots and women don't mix,' from this—whatsis name? Blakeslee. Blakeslee had clobbered the female vanity of America. Debden, when it saw the clipping, was one big belly laugh. 'Look who's talking!' they roared.

"Blakeslee returned to Debden. First thing he did was to make a flat-footed denial that he had ever really said 'fighter pilots and women don't mix.' He now said: 'You can't fight the war without 'em.' This was a laugh, as everyone could remember having heard him mouth the first statement until it was a Debden cliché. For example, a few days before [Lt. Col James] Clark was to wed Lady Bridget-Elliot, daughter of a British earl, Blakeslee emitted an elaborate disquisition on just how the marriage would cost Clark to lose his vinegar. We assumed Blakeslee's disavowal of his favorite maxim grew out his sobering experience with the wounded girls who wrote him the biting letters. Later we learned the reason why Blakeslee was so purposeful, if not systematic, in disowning authorship. In the States he had been secretly wed to his old hometown girl."

Major James Goodson, USAF (Ret), formerly with the 4th Fighter Group, Eighth USAAF, at Debden, had his doubts about "fighter pilots and women" in wartime: "Marriage tempered a man too much and the cau-

JANES

Women pilots of the British Air Transport Authority on a Spitfire in wartime England.

tious pilot is doomed. I've never seen a fighter pilot get married and keep on the way he was. He gets careful, thinking about his wife. The first thing you know he's thinking about her and a Hun bounces his tail."

It was the girls in the services who figured most immediately in the lives of the Allied fighter pilots. Driver, plotter, or nurse, the girls in uniform were often more than just that to the fliers. Friendships and romances flourished between the pilots and the girls working together on the same stations.

A portion of one of Major John T. Godfrey's combat reports sets the scene for an encounter on the evening of March 21, 1944: "VF-P—White Three—Fighter sweep into Bordeaux. Weather wasn't so hot so went under clouds at 20,000 feet all the way from Bordeaux to two aerodromes south of Rouen. We went down to strafe and I was hit by a 40mm. Bad scare. Group destroyed twenty-one Jerries. Time—3:50.

"I climbed out of my Mustang and walked over to Larry [his crew chief], who was standing there gaping at the huge hole to the rear of the cockpit. We walked silently around the plane, and on the other side we saw where the shell had entered before exploding. Larry put his thumb by the hole and spread out his fingers; I knew what he meant. If the shell had entered four inches forward, instead of just in the back of my armor-plated seat, it would have exploded in the cockpit and blown me to smithereens! He unscrewed the section which held the radio and, reaching in, brought out jagged pieces of metal. How lucky can a fellow get! Only one piece of the exploding shell had hit me. There was a small wound on my right knee, from which a small bit of shrapnel protrud-

ed—my only injury.

"'Say, Doc, can you put a real big bandage around that little cut? I want to play a joke on someone.'

"The doctor had just removed some German steel from my knee, with tweezers. Now he kept on bandaging until I had a knee as big as a football.

"'Now will you call up the tent hospital and see if you can arrange for Lieutenant Charlotte Fredericks to change the dressing around, let's see, eight o'clock tonight?'

"The doc fixed me up, and at eight that evening I was limping horribly as Charlotte held me by the arm on our way to the dressing room.

"'I don't know why they picked on me, but seeing you're here, don't expect any other treatment but medicinal.'

"'Yes, ma'am.'

"I thought it was all a big joke, until I realized with embarrassment that I would have to take my pants down—wouldn't pull up over the large bandage. I thought I caught a wry smile on her face when she held a white sheet in front of me as I dropped my trousers. I moaned horribly as I sat down and straightened my leg. I wanted to make this last, so I told her of the agonies I had suffered flying all the way from France with my mangled leg, weak from loss of the blood which nearly filled the cockpit.

"Very gently she started to unwrap and unwrap until the floor was littered with the bandage. She didn't say a word when she came to the cut; she just took a Band-Aid out of her pocket. Laughing in spite of herself, she said, 'Don't think you're so smart. The doctor's my friend, too. I was going to give you hypo, but if you promise to behave yourself I just might let you buy me a drink.'

"'Well, if you don't stand around

gaping at me while I put my pants back on I just might do that.'

"I made progress that night—we held hands, but only after a few drinks.'"

"A Polish pilot, older than the rest of us, had been a pre-war regular officer in the Polish air force. He had fought in France and then joined the RAF after Dunkirk. There was a girl in Scotland, Margaret, who he was close friends with and with whom he spent his leave.

"It fell to me one day to tell him he was to be sent on a rest tour. He protested at this, and I told him he had done his share and deserved a rest. I told him to go and visit Margaret, and that he was not as young as he once was. He thought about that and said: 'Perhaps so. I used to fly all day and sleep with girls all night. Now, when I fly all day and sleep with the girls all night, sometimes in the morning I feel a bit tired.'"
—Flight Lieutenant Douglas Warren, RCAF (Ret), formerly with Nos 66 and 165 Squadrons

The girls in the American airplane "nose art" of World War II England were never dressed for the cold altitudes where the airplanes flew. Some were scantily clad, more were nudes but coyly posed, and some were front-view nudes, bold and biologically complete.

The girls most popular in barracks pin-up photos were Betty Grable, who had legs; Lana Turner, who was the "Sweater Girl"; Dorothy Lamour, who wore sarongs; Mae West, after whose bulging balcony an inflatable life-jacket had been named; and Rita Hayworth, in a shot of her arising from bedcovers like Aphrodite from the ocean foam. The most desirable calendar art was the airbrush work of

Assistant Section Officer Edith Heap of Britain's Auxilliary Air Force. She joined the WAAF in 1939 as an MT driver, later became an operations room plotter and, finally, an intelligence officer debriefing RAF bomber crews. Her fiancé, Pilot Officer Denis Wissler, a Battle of Britain pilot, was killed in action on November 11, 1940.

two artists named Petty and Vargas, whose nudes were shown in poses and proportions as seductive on paper as they would have been grotesque in life.

But the place of honor among these pin-ups was occupied by shots of the Girl Back Home, whose one-time reality was maintained only through correspondence. Much time was spent in writing long and often torrid letters to her. Letters from her were the highlight of mail call—unless one of them happened to be a Dear John, telling the crestfallen recipient he had been replaced in her affections, causing him to suffer days of black depression usually accompanied by a monumental binge.

The American Red Cross girls ran the base Aero Club, which, but for its lack of a bar, was to enlisted men what the officers' club was to officers. Also, in a van called a "clubmobile," the Red Cross girls took coffee and doughnuts to work crews around the base and to pilots at debriefings. They were difficult to date, causing some enlisted men to complain that Red Cross girls had eyes only for officers. The problem, however, was simply that they were so few among thousands of men. Accordingly, most dating, by both enlisted men and officers, was with local girls, who were not difficult to date at all.

"They are loose as a goose," wrote one pilot in his diary, "and outspoken about what they will give you for gum or candy." He wrote those words, however, after only six days in England, and had not yet learned that in percentages of "loose as a goose," prim and proper, and somewhere in between, English girls were not too different from those in the States. The great influx of troops, though,

did cause a sharp increase in English membership of the "oldest profession."

When Mae West saw an item in a Los Angeles newspaper suggesting that the name "Mae West" for the RAF life-saving jacket might soon get into the dictionary, she wrote the following letter to *Tee Emm*, the wartime RAF magazine:
"Dear Boys of the RAF,

"I have just seen that the RAF flyers have a life-saving jacket they call a 'Mae West,' because it bulges in all the 'right places.' Well, I consider it a swell honor to have such great guys wrapped up in you, know what I mean?

"Yes, it's kind of a nice thought to be flying all with brave men . . . even if I'm only there by proxy in the form of a life-saving jacket, or a life-saving jacket in my form.

"I always thought that the best way to hold a man was in your arms—but I guess when you're up in the air a plane is safer. You've got to keep everything under control.

"Yeah, the jacket idea is all right, and I can't imagine anything better than to bring you boys of the RAF soft and happy landings. But what I'd like to know about the life-saving jacket is—has it got dangerous curves and soft shapely shoulders?

"You've heard of Helen of Troy, the dame with the face that launched a thousand ships . . . why not a shape that will stop thousands of tanks?

"If I do get in the dictionary— where you say you want to put me—how will they describe me? As a warm and clinging life-saving garment worn by aviators? Or an aviator's jacket that supplies the woman's touch while the boys are flying around nights? How would you describe me, boys?

"I've been in Who's Who, and I

Young female guests on an American fighter station in England during WWII are served a meal by a mess sergeant.

know what's what, but it'll be the first time I ever made the dictionary.
"Sin-sationally,
Mae West"

For the pilots of No 238 Squadron, RAF, a favorite local was the Square Club at Andover, Hampshire. It was populated with groupies of the time who directed their attentions toward the airmen of 238. One of these ladies, known to the pilots as "The Gypsy," had long black hair, wore full skirts, and flaunted her curvy shape and excellent legs. During the Battle of Britain the average pilot's life expectancy was brief, but those the Gypsy favored tended to last only a few days. Talk about fatal charms . . . more than once a pilot she slept with was shot down the next day. There was speculation that she was an enemy agent who doped the drinks of her pilot friends to foul their flying skills.

"I was tired and dirty when I arrived at the mess. In the bar I could hear sounds of merriment, but I was in no mood for it. I just needed bed. I should at least have washed, but I was too tired for that even. I went into the dining room. It was silent and in darkness, so I pushed through the swing doors into forbidden territory, the kitchens. My 'hello' produced an answer from amidst the ranges and sinks. It was a WAAF who answered me, standing near a range with one shoe on. The other shoe was poised in her left hand. In her right she held a blacking brush.

"Obviously, she was 'bulling up' her shoes. 'Who is the Duty Cook?' I asked. 'Right here', she replied. 'Are you the Operational Breakfast?' My affirmative produced an immediate reaction. She dropped the shoe brush, pulled a mob cap over her upswept

hair, and at the same time did a hop and a skip toward the hot range, pushing a large frying pan over the heat. She had her back to me and I was faintly amused at the girl. One shoe on and one shoe off, with wisps of mousy brown hair sticking out from the back of her cap.

"It was a stupid thing to do, as fraternization between officers and WAAFs was frowned upon, but I pushed her loose hair back under her hat. She stiffened as I gazed at her slender white neck disappearing into a white overall. She wore no shirt. Round her neck was a gold chain with a small cross resting at the top of her bosom. She turned to look at me. I must have looked terrible, as an oxygen mask always left its outline of dirt around nose and mouth.

"She lifted her face and swung her arms around my neck, one hand still holding a black shoe. We kissed. It was a long, warm kiss and I felt the blood run hot in my chest.

"Before I could repeat the operation, there was the sound of footsteps beyond the swing doors. We broke away from each other like naughty children. I turned toward the dining room and she to the frying pan. I was sitting in semi-darkness in the deserted dining room when she came in with a plate which she put before me. 'That was nice,' I said. 'Lovely,' she replied, wrinkling her nose and turning away. I could hear distant laughter from the bar as I picked up a knife and fork. I glanced down at the plate. 'Oh, good,' I thought. 'Two eggs!' That was the thing about WAAFs. Whatever the job, they never stopped being women."
—Pilot Officer Nick Berryman, RAF (Ret), formerly with No 276 Squadron

"Men love war because it allows them to look serious. Because it is

the one thing that stops women laughing at them."
—from *The Magus* by John Fowles

"I am sitting in a bus traveling narrow country roads bordered by green hedgerows. My husband sits beside me. We are in the part of England known as East Anglia, midmorning on a bright Saturday. I am one of fourteen wives on the bus, watching both the scenery outside and the unfolding drama inside.

"Our husbands, some with thinning gray hair, some with slightly arthritic limbs, several with vials of heart medicine tucked handily in their pockets, lean forward in their seats, peering out the bus windows through the tops of their bifocals—excited and anxious as little boys. Each wears a specially-ordered cap with 353rd Fighter Group, Eighth Air Force, printed on the front. They are looking for what's left of Raydon Airfield where they lived for two long, lonesome years during World War II.

"I say, it must be near here, says our travel agent in dignified British English. (The 1984 maps of England do not show old World War II airfields.)

"'Look!' Suddenly, one of the men points toward a bulky, black shadow looming against a blue horizon. 'That's a hangar!'

"'That has to be Raydon,' says another voice with a funny catch. Our visit had been carefully planned, even written up in the village newspaper. First we are to stop at the Peabody farm. Mr. Peabody now owns most of the land that was once Raydon airfield.

"'Welcome back to Raydon,' Peabody says as he boards the bus. 'As you can see, there is no longer an airfield here, but more of Raydon survives than most World War II airfields.

Jitterbugging at one of many dances hosted by fighter and bomber groups of the Eighth USAAF on their wartime bases in England.

left: Red Cross girls offering coffee and doughnuts to weary USAAF personnel on an airbase in southern England during WWII; above: The Wolf Wagon bus used to bring local girls to the Leiston base of the 357FG for parties and dances during the war.

I'd like to show you about.'

"The big bus pulls onto blacktop road and stops amid a cluster of metal Quonset-type buildings. These are the remaining buildings, now used by the government. And here, too, is the big black hangar.

"The men are out among the buildings. The three who were pilots head toward the hangar, those who were mechanics, armorers, and radiomen head toward other buildings. I follow my husband, who walks with his friend, Charley Graham, on the remains of the runway.

"Weeds are growing through the cracks in the old cement.

"'Remember when we were standing right here when Colonel Ben's plane crashed,' Charley says.

"Slowly the men drift back toward the bus. I sense a sort of sadness, a letdown. Is this really Raydon? Are these few old buildings in the middle of a farm field all that's left to show for the years spent here? So long ago, the memories faint. Was it real—that war?

"Reluctantly, they board the bus. Then, from a farm beyond the lane a woman calls to us. 'Wait! Wait!' She runs toward the bus holding something in her hand. She reaches the group, breathless and laughing. 'Forty years ago when you were here I was a little girl living on my father's farm. One of you hit a baseball over the fence into our farmyard. I found it, but I didn't throw it back. I kept it all these years.' She smiles sheepishly. 'When I read you were coming, I thought you'd want to see it.'

"The men gather around her, laughing, each holding the old baseball for a moment, then passing it on. They need that baseball. Somehow it proves that Raydon was real, that the 353rd Fighter Group was here—and that the men were young and vital and strong enough to hit a baseball way over into that farmyard.

"We thank her and climb back onto the bus. There is a spirit of joy now.

"On to town. Two hundred people live in Raydon. Most of them are here to celebrate the day with us. There are races and games in the schoolyard. Inside a potluck supper is waiting: chicken pies, Cornish pasties, potted shrimp. 'You are the first group to come back,' they tell us.

"The next morning we dress in our best clothes. The bus takes us to the tiny Anglican church built in the year 1200 and packed to capacity this Sunday morning. The Americans sit together in the front. When the service ends, Charley Graham stands and asks to say a word. 'We have a gift for you.' He holds the check, our collective gift. 'We have 1,000 American dollars to be spent in any way you choose. We ask only one thing—that a little of it be spent for a plaque in this church remembering the men of the 353rd Fighter Group who served at Raydon—so that our grandchildren, when they come to visit, will know that we were here.'

"There is silence in the ancient church; the organ begins to play the 'Star-Spangled Banner.' I look down the rows and see tears on every cheek. How strange life is, I think. An old baseball brought those long-ago days back to life, and a little plaque will keep them living.

"We walk from the cool stone church into the bright morning. We say good-bye and board the bus. —Eudora Seyfer, wife of George A. Seyfer, formerly an armorer with the 353rd Fighter Group, Eighth USAAF

In late 1991 the United States Senate voted overwhelmingly to overturn a forty-three-year-old law that barred women from flying warplanes in combat. The measure was an amendment to the military budget bill for the 1992 fiscal year. It would permit, but would not require, the air force, the navy, the army, and the marine corps to allow women to fly combat missions. The House of Representatives had already approved similar legislation and Defense Secretary Dick Cheney indicated that he did not oppose the provision. The measure was sponsored by Senator Bill Roth, Republican of Delaware, and Senator Edward Kennedy, Democrat of Massachusetts. The action was a "victory for the women pilots who demonstrated in the Gulf their patriotism, courage and competence," Kennedy said.

left: Wounded Luftwaffe fighter pilot Oscar Boesch and his girlfriend during his wartime service; below: In the crew room of the 336FS, 4FG at Debden, England, in 1944.

GUARDIANS

Members of the 4FG in a mission briefing at Debden in WWII.

A KEY ROLE of the Allied fighter pilot in World War II was to shepherd his "big friends"—the bombers—to and from their targets in the various theaters of war. He did this with moderate success for a while, but it was the advent of the ultra-long-range Mustang fighter that ultimately made the difference in the strategic bombing campaigns.

One who flew the Mustang on the escort missions of the 357th Fighter Group from its Leiston, England, base was Captain William Overstreet, USAF (Ret): "It's funny how different a mission is after you've completed a few dozen. At first, everything is exciting—having the CQ wake you, eating your powdered eggs (usually green), going to the briefing room and seeing the tape across the map. So that's where we are going today. How many German planes will come up to intercept the bombers and us? How good are the flak gunners? Will we have a chance to go down and do some strafing? You make your notes to put on your knee pad so you have the vital information. When and where do we rendezvous with the bombers? What is the proper heading and how long will it take at X miles per hour? How strong is the wind and from what direction? I know some fellas who have been blown so far off course that they didn't have enough gas to get back to England.

"Now, let us get all of our equipment: mike, oxygen mask, Mae West, raft, parachute and all of the other things we may need. Climb on a weapons carrier for a ride out to my plane. It stops in front of my *Berlin Express* and I am greeted by Red Dodsworth and Whitey McKain. They are part of the crew who take care of my plane and make sure that everything is in the best shape possible. They have worked long and hard and inform me that the plane runs smooth

as a kitten. I hope it can be a real tiger as well.

"It is time to start the planes. As usual, the weather is so poor that they want a crew chief to ride the wing and help guide me while I taxi out to the runway. Whitey is sitting on my wing, and after the engine is running I leave the pad to follow Andy's [Captain Clarence E. Anderson] plane. I get to fly Andy's wing today, so I know I will be with the best. He is already an ace and really helps all of the pilots gain confidence and be better in combat. I got to fly a lot with him while training in

P-39s, and now, in our best fighter, the P-51, no one can outfly us.

"I have my canopy nearly closed to keep the snow out and feel sorry for Whitey out on the wing in the snowstorm. But, with his help, I make it to the end of the runway and pull up beside Andy's *Old Crow*. He is on the left side of the runway and I am on the right a few feet away and a few feet behind him. I wave for Whitey to leave and I concentrate on Andy.

"Now I am in the air, climbing in the clouds, staying as close to Andy as I can because if I lose sight of him for an instant, I will be on my own in that

cloud that I have to climb through before I can see anything or anybody again. I remember two friends who had a midair collision under these same circumstances and neither lived through it. That gives me enough incentive to stay close.

"Today we are lucky, as we break out of the clouds at about 7,000 feet, and soon the rest of the squadron is breaking out and forming up in flights of four. At full strength, each squadron would have four flights of four, and the group would have three squadrons. This time we don't have enough planes and pilots so we have only

left: One of the "Big Friends" that were escorted by the USAAF fighters in the round-the-clock bombing offensive against Germany; below: The derelict control tower at RAF Bovingdon.

three flights and one spare from our squadron. This works out just right, as Irving Smith calls on the radio. 'Sorry fellas, my engine is too rough. I have to abort.' So the spare man, Ernest Tiede, moves up to take Smith's place. Now Irv has the fun of looking for our base in the heavy clouds, with a rough engine.

"We continue climbing and heading for Muritz Lake where we are to meet the bombers at 12:40. Andy has me for his wingman, with Joe Pierce and Bill Michaely as his element. We have all flown together for some time in P-39s and P-51s, so we settle in for nearly two hours of cold, uncomfortable sitting in the tight confines of our planes, on constant alert as the enemy could try to surprise us at any time. All he has to do is climb up into the sun and wait for a chance to pounce on us, as their radar gives them the information they need about where we are and what direction we are heading. That is why most missions are set in some general direction and then adjusted toward the specific target of the day. We try to keep them guessing if we can.

"We find the bombers just a few minutes late and in a somewhat loose formation. Our three squadrons take up their positions—one on the right—one on the left—and we are the high squadron for today. That means we stay above the bombers and, after checking to be sure the German fighters don't have a high cover to jump us, we can dive to get more speed and break up any enemy formations that try to attack the bombers. We gently weave at reduced speed so we can hold our positions with the bombers who are slower than us.

"Soon Andy calls, 'Bogies at twelve o'clock—get ready to drop tanks.' He

has sighted enemy fighters straight ahead of us and we should turn our fuel switches from our wing tanks so we can drop them and prepare for combat. Now we really get apprehensive. All of our training, everything we know, is going to be put to the test. The Germans still have lots of good pilots and planes, and about forty of us are going to try to chase off about two hundred of them who are willing to do anything to keep our bombers from getting over their factories, refineries, or any other prime targets in their homeland.

"We drop our wing tanks, give the planes more throttle, and head for the German formation. They are lined up in waves of about twenty abreast so that they can go through the bombers and use all their guns and cannon with plenty of targets for each of them.

"Andy picks out the one who seems to be their leader and goes after him. I ease back a little so I can watch behind Andy's plane and make sure that no one can get behind him. If a fighter can get behind another plane, his guns are much more accurate than at a wider deflection shot from other positions. That is why we always try to get on the enemy's tail, and try to avoid letting them get behind us. A good fighter group is a team. Each man has his job and if everyone does his job well, the team effort is successful. My job is to make sure that, while Andy is trying to get behind the enemy, none of them gets in position behind him.

"By now the other squadrons have joined the attack. Try to imagine about forty P-51s and two hundred Me 109s and Fw 190s in a mad scramble with each pilot trying to shoot down any of the enemy planes he can get a shot at while making sure they are kept away from gaining position on our planes. Throttles are pushed forward for maximum power, and as fast as we can go we are in circles, climbing, diving, rolling . . . any possible maneuver to get a shot at them while they are trying to do the same to us. I see Andy get hits on several of them and I get a burst at a 109 that got too close to getting behind Andy. When he felt my .50 caliber rounds hit his tail, he dove for the deck to get away from us.

"The scramble is really getting wild. All our planes are chasing German fighters, and breaking away when they get in position behind us. That means making a fast turn to keep him from having a good shot at us. It seems that the sky is full of planes in every conceivable position, frequently inverted, and I am firing whenever I think I am in position to get some hits.

"We have succeeded in diverting most of the enemy but a few have got through and hit the bombers. By now, a lot of planes are smoking— some of our bombers and some of their fighters—and parachutes are blossoming below us as people leave their crippled planes.

"After what seems an eternity, but is actually only about five or ten minutes, the remaining bombers are still heading for their target and our fighters are now chasing any German fighters that haven't dived for the deck to get out of the fight. While most of our planes are scattered, Andy and I are still together and the element, Joe and Bill, is still nearby. Andy sees some German fighters getting ready to hit the bombers again, so we head for them. Andy comes up below and behind a 109 and closes to within a few hundred yards. I keep thinking he can fire, but he waits until he is about 100 yards out and pulls the trigger. There is an explosion. The right wing falls off and the enemy pilot decides

left: Captain William O'Brien in his P-51C Mustang at Leiston; above: Major Fred Christensen of the 56FG, Eighth USAAF, in 1944.

he had better walk home. He leaves the plane with his parachute while I fire at his wingman. Sparkles light up on the fuselage and tail. He flips over and dives for the deck. Joe has convinced another German to leave his plane by setting his engine on fire.

"Now targets aren't as plentiful, but we see ten German fighters still trying to get to the bombers. They see us coming and decide to head for home. We decide to go after them. We follow them in a power dive, pushing the airspeed indicator to the red line. When you go from 25,000 feet to the deck in a hurry, you are

fighting trim tabs, rudders, and everything else to keep flying straight. We all manage and Andy is closing on one of their planes when the pilot pulls back on the stick and tries to lose us by climbing. Andy stays right with him and I stay with Andy, just a little later. The German starts every evasive tactic he can, but when he and Andy are upside down, Andy gets a burst into the German's engine and that is that. With his engine on fire, he also elects to walk home.

"Now we are a few thousand feet over Germany, the German planes are scattered in all directions, and when we followed them our group was all over the map. A decision has to be made—do we go back up to see if we can help any bombers who may have lost engines and can't keep up with their formation? They are sitting ducks for enemy fighters, so some P-51s escorting them could make the difference to their survival. Or shall we stay on the deck and look for trains, barges, ammunition dumps, or military convoys?

"As we are low on ammunition, we start climbing. Soon, Joe and Bill join us, and after all of the action, our flight is together to start back to England, offering assistance to any 'wounded' bombers we see as long as our fuel holds out. We try to avoid the areas of heavy flak. In some places German gunners can turn the sky black with exploding bursts.

"We stay with a bomber that has lost two engines until we approach the English Channel and we feel they can make it. We have just enough fuel to get back. There are still a lot of clouds over England, but now the ceiling is almost 100 feet so we have no trouble getting to our base and landing.

"There is no way anyone could count the planes we shot at, or who shot at us, or the number of ground gunners with good radar firing at us. How many times did we have an enemy plane in our sights, but had to break it off because an enemy plane was closing behind us? How many times did we have to break off to chase one who was closing in on one of our teammates? A dogfight is almost a blur because of the fast and furious action. Today went into the books as a mission of a little over five hours, with us destroying sixteen German planes, while one of our pilots had to bail out over Germany. I am awfully glad to be back."

"The worst escort I had to fly was against England in June 1940, from Coquelles near Calais. The order was a direct escort for Ju 87s, the dive-bomber, heavy, slow, and unmaneuverable. So, we gave up all our advantages and the Spitfires just waited for us upstairs. We had big losses and the tactics were changed. Certainly, escort is a primary mission for a fighter, but he has to have the freedom of moving and

below: A P-47 Thunderbolt pilot of the 56FG at Boxted, England, in the Second World War; right: The remains of the control tower at Deenethorpe, England.

selecting his position in the air."
—Generalleutnant a.D. Günther Rall, German air force (Ret)

Oberleutnant Dirk Wiegmann was a Navigator/Weapons System Officer with 1/AG51 of the German air force since early in 1995: "On our recce missions, we try to protect ourselves with our weapons, but we have our escort . . . our own fighters flying with us and we pretty much count on them. They try to keep us free from enemy fighters, and if this doesn't work, we try to run away. That's our actual role in the Tornado. We can't really fight with the aircraft. It's not built for that. It's built for taking pictures or delivering bombs, not to fight against a third-generation fighter. There is no chance. In that situation, we just drop everything and run away, if possible."

"In my first tour we did a lot of escort work, which was frustrating as we were flying the Spitfire Mk Vs, which were no match for the Fw 190s. It was really difficult to keep position on the slower bombers. Free-ranging area escort, with good ground control, is more effective. My opinion is that it is better to fly fighters than bombers. We saw our share of bombers brought down by flak and couldn't do anything about it."
—Flight Lieutenant Douglas Warren, RCAF (Ret), formerly with Nos 66 and 165 Squadrons, RAF

Carroll "Red" McColpin was born in Buffalo, New York. A pilot since 1928, he volunteered for the Royal Air Force in November 1940 and was the only American to fly in combat with all three Eagle Squadrons. He commanded No 133 (Eagle) Squadron until it transferred to the Eighth USAAF in September 1942, becoming part of the 4th Fighter Group at Debden, Essex, England. Red McColpin was officially credited with 11.5 kills, four probably destroyed, twelve damaged (all aerial), plus numerous aircraft, tanks, trucks, and boats destroyed. He was awarded twenty-nine decorations from five governments, and two Presidential Unit Citations. He retired from the U.S. Air Force in 1968 with the rank of major general.

"We met them over England . . . thirty-six B-26s [medium bombers], and they went on over Belgium in bright sunlight. We were all around them. They went in and there was Liege and the river there, and the bridges across the Rhine. They were to bomb these bridges. We were sitting up there looking at the sky and at them too, and pretty soon, I said, 'You know, you're getting awfully close to your target. It's just ahead of you, to the left.' No answer. Then, finally, someone in the bomber formation said, 'We know where we're goin'.' And they flew on by their IP [the initial point in a bombing run]. Well, with no IP, they don't know how to bomb, so they go all the way around again, and all this time with flak all over the place. They go all the way back out to Brussels and they turned south again . . . got on course again to hit the IP and make another [bomb] run. This time they got up to the IP, and then turned. I guess they thought they didn't see the right bridge. I thought, Jesus, they've got it this time' . . . and they flew right past it, and all the way out to Brussels again, and in again. And this time I said, 'I don't know what your problem is, but if you'll just continue on that course for three minutes or so, turn left and there are the bridges.' And the guy says, 'Stop trying to talk us into the target.' And I said, 'It's your target, dammit!' And they missed it again. They go all the way back out to Brussels again, and I said, 'I'm real sorry, but I've got fifty-two guys here and we don't have enough fuel for you to do this again, 'cause if you do it one more time and then we're jumped at that point, we ain't gonna get home. So I suggest you figure out something else 'cause we're leaving you when we get to the coast.' And they said, 'Well, we're on our way home anyway.' And they went out over the coast ten or fifteen miles off of Brussels . . . and all of them jettisoned their bombs and went on home."

Red McColpin knew that Morlaix, a

big mission, was coming up: "But I'd been ordered to transfer to the Eighth USAAF. Ordered. I kept delaying it, week after week, We were down at Biggin Hill, but 133 [Eagle] Squadron was being moved up to Great Sampford, near Debden. The mission was being laid on . . . then off . . . then on again. I decided I wouldn't go and leave the outfit until the mission was over with. I was gonna lead the mission. Then General 'Mink' Hunter called me from Fighter Command Headquarters of the Eighth Air Force, and said, 'I understand you haven't transferred,' and I said, 'Yes, sir.' He just said, 'Well, you get your butt in there and transfer, right now!' To

which I came back, 'Sir, I'm waiting for this Morlaix mission and I'm trying to keep enough boys in here to run it, 'cause it's a big one.' 'To heck with that. You get in there and transfer,' Hunter replied. 'Well, sir,' I said, 'you understand that I'm in the Royal Air Force, and I have an Ops instruction here which says we are going to Morlaix when they lay it on. I'm the CO here, and I've got my squadron on the line.' With that, he snorted and hung up. About an hour later I got a call from an air marshal in the group. 'McColpin, do you take orders from me?' I said, 'I certainly do, sir.' That's how I came to transfer over."

The Morlaix raid, when it came, was

a disaster, and proved a sad way for the Eagle Squadrons to bow out of the RAF. Gordon Brettell, a British pilot, was placed in command of 133 Squadron, and led the mission, on September 26, 1942, in Red McColpin's place.

The Morlaix raid required the Eagles to escort American B-17 bombers hitting the Brest Peninsula, flying out across the widest part of the English Channel, over a heavily defended area, and back again. By this time, 133 Squadron was at Great Sampford in Essex, waiting to be absorbed into the U.S. Army Air Force, but still was to fly the Morlaix mission. The unit was sent to Bolt Head, a forward base located

left: Nissen huts at the former Steeple Morden base near Cambridge; above: The perimeter track at Raydon airfield.

between Dartmouth and Plymouth in Devon. Here its pilots were to refuel, be briefed for the mission, and join the other two squadrons flying it, Nos 401 and 412 (Canadian). On the flight down to Bolt Head, the weather was bad and getting worse, threatening the impending mission.

Without McColpin's discipline, the pilots of 133 Squadron were overly casual in preparing for Morlaix. Most did not even bother to attend the briefing. Only Brettell and one other pilot were briefed for the raid. In it the Met officer gave a tragically erroneous piece of information—a predicted thirty-five-knot headwind at the mission height of 28,000 feet. Further, no one knew precisely when the bombers were to takeoff, or their precise rendezvous time with the fighters. The pilots lounged under the wings of their Spitfires and waited. McColpin's key word, planning, certainly did not apply. The takeoff was a mess. There were near-collisions; pilots did not get proper instructions about radio channels; some even left maps and escape kits behind.

Flying with auxiliary fuel tanks, thirty-six Spitfires headed out to meet the bombers. There was no sign of them, and the fighters continued on course and called by radio for news of their "big friends." The predicted thirty-five-knot headwind had been a major miscalculation. Both bombers and fighters—miles apart—were being whisked along by a 100-knot tailwind. One of the pilots later commented: "It all added up to a streaking catastrophe." Miles ahead of the fighters, the bombers had unknowingly crossed the Bay of Biscay above a blanket of cloud and, on reaching the Pyrenees mountains, discovered their problem, dumped their bombs, and swung back to the north on a reciprocal course, meeting the Spitfires head-

left: The cockpit of a Mustang under restoration at Duxford; above: The wallet of an Eighth USAAF fighter pilot lost in WWII.

Colonel Vermont Garrison was one of only seven Americans to achieve ace status during WWII and again in the Korean War; right: Four American fighter pilots heading for their planes; below right: P-51 Mustangs in finger-four formation over England in WWII.

on. The fighters turned north as well. By this time, all the aircraft had vanished from the radar plots in England, and communications between bombers, fighters, and their various bases was a shambles.

Having been airborne for two hours and fifteen minutes, the Spitfire pilots believed they were near home again and began to let down through the cloud cover. A coastline appeared, which they assumed to be England. It was, in fact, the French coast, and they passed over Brest harbor and through a massive flak barrage. In moments ten Spitfires were lost, four pilots killed, and six downed and captured, among them the CO, Gordon Brettell. Two other Spitfires failed to return to Bolt Head. Morlaix was a most unfortunate final mission for the Eagles.

The Ready Room bulletin board of the 351st Fighter Squadron, 353rd Fighter Group at Raydon, Suffolk, near the eastern coast of England: In 1944 it showed Lieutenant Robert Strobell and his fellow pilots the names of those who would fly in combat each day: "If your name was not on the combat board, you could be assured that you would be assigned to other flying chores such as 'slow-timing' an airplane that had had a new engine installed, much like breaking in a new car engine. Or you might be assigned to a plane that was having turbo supercharger problems and a test flight had to be made to 30,000 feet to test the adjustment or repair. Or you might be asked to take a plane to the depot inland for major repairs, train a new replacement pilot on instruments, dive-bombing, rat races, navigation, or simply test-hop a plane that had been running rough before repairs or adjustments had been done. It was in the Ready Room that you got these assignments.

The crew of the B-17 *Buckeye Belle*, 384BG, Grafton Underwood on March 19, 1945; above: The sign of the The Flying Fortress pub at Rougham, near Bury St. Edmunds in Suffolk, England.

B-17 bombers of the Horham-based 95BG,
and their escort of P-47 Thunderbolt fighters.

"The room was set up theater-style facing a very large map of most of England, the English Channel and most of western Europe. I recall that the map was almost always covered when we entered the room for briefing—I assume for security purposes. The map always had two colored lines on it, one for the bombers and another color for our route and support, showing where we would rendezvous with the bombers. Whenever the mission lines showed deep penetration into Germany, you could hear some muttering and cussing among the pilots as soon as the curtain went up. Off to one side of the map there was a bulletin board with large letters and numbers on it, readable from the back of the room. This board had the time of takeoff, the combat altitude that we would fly, the compass heading to rendezvous, the time that we would stay on escort with the bombers, and the compass heading for the return portion of the mission. We were briefed on the weather over the mission area and the forecast for the base upon our return, the bombers' mission, enemy movements if any, and sometimes a brief comment on what some of the other squadrons had done the day before. It was obvious that a lot of time and effort went into the planning and presentation of these briefings.

"While sleeping in the Nissen hut, you didn't have to be concerned about waking at a specific hour. You simply went to sleep knowing that an orderly would come through and wake you and tell you the time that you were due in the Ready Room. You jumped out of bed, hit the latrine, dressed and walked to the Ready Room. There you would find your assignment for the day posted on the board. If it was a combat mission, you would attend the briefing right after breakfast. Following the

The German-occupied airfield of Denain/Prouvy in France, after an attack by bombers of the American Eighth Air Force in July 1944, as photographed by a reconnaissance fighter of the 7th Photo Group.

briefing, most of us hit the latrine again, some in panic and others out of necessity. Then you picked up your parachute and went outside where there was a personnel-type truck with a canvas cover and bench seats on each side, to take you and the other pilots out to the revetments, dropping pilots at their airplanes as it proceeded around the perimeter of the field. There you would find your crew chief waiting. He had been alerted many hours before as to the times of the flight and which planes would be flying that day. This was done on the telephone, conference-style, to all squadrons, so that the orders for the day only had to be read once. The crew chief briefed you on the status of the plane, usually 'ready' for combat, and warned you about the minor glitches such as a tail-wheel shimmy. Then he helped you climb up on the wing, don your parachute (some did this on the ground), and settle into the cockpit. He helped you with the shoulder harness and seat belt. If it was a combat mission, you usually sat in the airplane for a few minutes, or even a half hour, waiting for a signal to start your engine. Since you already knew what your position was in the flight, and on whose wing you were flying, you taxied out to the taxi strip in that position when your leader came by, and you would both take off, side-by-side, on each side of the runway. Then it was off into the wild blue, complete the mission, come home and taxi back to the same revetment. You would tell your crew chief what you did on that mission, and most importantly, what the airplane did or did not do, and what needed to be repaired, or if you had any battle damage, bullet holes, or flak hits . . . that is, if you knew about them . . . some pilots didn't know they had been hit. Then you hopped into a jeep or truck that

left: The massive U-boat pen shelters on the Brittany coast of France were a prime target for the bombers of the Eighth USAAF in WWII. This one is at Brest; above: Bomb damage to one of the immense pen structures.

A P-51 Mustang, one of the "Little Friends" that guarded the American bomber stream to and from its targets deep in Germany; right: Colonel Don Blakeslee commanded the 4FG in early 1944 when it was converted from the P-47 Thunderbolt to the Mustang.

took you back to the Ready Room. If you had fired your guns on the mission, the Intelligence Officer wanted to see you for a debriefing, particularly on enemy encounters, in which you had fired on an enemy aircraft in the air or on the ground. The whole process, from beginning to end, took from four to as much as eight hours, depending on the length of the mission and the complexity of the operation. Back in the Ready Room you learned if you were scheduled to fly another mission, the second of the day. During my six months at Raydon, I flew two combat missions in one day ten times.

"There were physical problems for

A superbly restored Mustang at an air show,
Duxford, England.

some of the pilots. The most painful was the sinus block from head colds. No problem climbing up to altitude. But on the way back to base, over the Channel as you let down, if your sinuses blocked up it felt like someone hit you in the forehead with a sledge-hammer. The only choice you had was to climb back up high enough to relieve the pain and start blowing and praying that it wouldn't block again on the way down. On one long flight into Germany, I had a hip joint pop out. Not particularly painful, and my flight leader wondered why I was flopping around in the formation. This was caused by the seat belt putting pressure on my hip on a long flight. So physical problems could add a measure of stress to combat flying.

"Most pilots were uncomfortable in the cockpit because of the dinghy that they had to sit on. There was no way to pack a one-man dinghy so it would make a comfortable seat. The heavy rubber dinghy was packed in a square and mounted as the seat of the parachute pack. When you put on the parachute pack you had the dinghy next to your buttocks, with the parachute below it. It was far from being a cushion, and on a long flight it became almost unbearable. The dinghy was cussed by pilots, and you shifted and squirmed in the cockpit to relieve the butt numbness. The dinghy was appreciated only by those who went down in the sea. For everyone else, the discomfort added to the stress of flying.

"One might think that, with a year of training in navigation, cross-country flights, and weather studies, a replacement pilot would arrive at the squadron with confidence in his ability to fly over Europe in any kind of weather and find his way back to the base. Not so. Flying in heavy, solid, soggy weather was avoided in the States for safety reasons. I received more weather training from the 'old boys' after I got to the squadron than I did at any other station. You had to use your head in navigation, as well as your maps. Combining navigation and weather flying on the same flight demanded a bit of skill. Some pilots didn't have it, and it became a stressful situation for those who became separated from the squadron and had to make their own way home.

"On a number of combat missions time and distance became a matter of grave concern. Deep penetrations into Germany extended the P-47 to its maximum range. When you were in enemy territory and you knew you had reached the halfway point of the flight, you started to pray that you would not see or engage enemy fighters. To do so meant opening up the throttle and burning off large amounts of gasoline rapidly in a dogfight, leaving you without enough fuel to make it back to England.

"Much to my disappointment, the majority of combat missions during my tour were uneventful, because enemy aircraft were seldom encountered. Bomber escort missions were dull [then], as were the area support flights in France during the invasion, although I did get two air victories during this period. Combat flying is a lot of hard work, and there is certainly a stress factor.

"There is no sight more spectacular and impressive than the sun shining on the condensation trails of hundreds of fighters and bombers cross-hatching the sky. The bombers fly in a straight line for the most part, while the fighters hover over them, looping back and forth to stay with them at their slower speed. At altitude, 25,000 feet or more, these contrails may stretch clear across the Channel into Europe. It is a beautiful phenomenon, so large and changing each minute in shade and design . . . brilliant in the setting sun."

A few examples of the Eighth USAAF heavy bombers flying from English bases in WWII and protected by fighters of the Eighth Fighter Command.

RED STARS

WITH THE INVASION of the Soviet Union by Hitler's forces on June 22, 1941, everything changed for Soviet women aviators who had long wanted to fly in the military of their nation. The well-known female pilot and Hero of the Soviet Union, Marina Raskova, had been struggling for many months to form a women's aviation regiment, trying to persuade the government of the substantial contribution such units would provide to the war effort. Raskova was a high-achieving air navigator who, together with two other female aviators, had made many record-setting flights during the 1930s. The three were the first women to be awarded the coveted Hero of the Soviet Union and the only women to receive the honor prior to the Second World War. Their greatest achievement may have been the completion of a 1938 Moscow-Far East flight, breaking the women's international distance record. Their effort resulted in Joseph Stalin himself presenting their medals.

With the outbreak of the war, Marina Raskova formally petitioned the Soviet air force to establish, train and deploy women's regiments, but the petition became bogged down in a series of delays. The air force saw no need for additional pilots, having incurred some 7,500 aircraft losses in the first three months of the conflict, leaving the Soviets with far more pilots than aircraft. The general belief among veteran Soviet women aviators is that Raskova influenced Stalin through a personal appeal to see to the establishment of the units by the Air Force. With that decision made, and Stalin's apparently enthusiastic

The Russians called it the Great Patriotic War—
the rest of the world called it the Second World
War. Russian women were the only women in
the world to fly in combat during that conflict.

support, organization of the women's units moved swiftly, further motivated by the advancing German offensive on Moscow, Operation Typhoon, which began on September 30.

The organization of the female fliers began with an authorization for Raskova to form a temporary aviation group, the 122nd, to train women pilots, navigators, armorers, and mechanics; the group would ultimately become the basis for the formation of the 586th Fighter Aviation Regiment, the 587th Dive Bomber Regiment, and the 588th Night Bomber Regiment.

With the formation of these units, hundreds of Soviet women who had been trained as pilots before the war volunteered for the new units. Only those women with the highest qualifications—experienced instructors with the air clubs and with any civil or military background—were sought initially. Vitually none of them had had any training or experience as navigators or mechanics. Of the remainder, those with the highest levels of education, including many pilots, were accepted to train as mechanics, armorers, and for other ground roles.

Among the best-known of the Soviet women fighter pilots was Lilya Litvyak, who was an instructor when the war began, having already trained nearly fifty students. With the war, she immediately began applying for military duty, but was ordered to remain with her air club. Finally, she heard about Raskova's group, volunteered for it, and was accepted.

On October 16, the Raskova group traveled by train to the town of Engels, north of Stalingrad, where they were given initial military flight training and were then assigned to either fighters, day bombers, or night bombers.

The first lot of combat aircraft, Yak-1 fighters, were delivered to the

586th Fighter Aviation Regiment and were operational by April 1942. By September, one squadron from the 586th was detached and sent in support of two front-line regiments at Stalingrad. It consisted of eight women pilots and their female mechanics and armorers. Their transfer orders were received on September 10. On the 13th, one of their number, Lilya Litvyak, became the first woman in history to shoot down an enemy aircraft when she downed two in a day. Her friend and mechanic, Inna Pasportnikova, recalled: "The situation both on the ground and in the air at Stalingrad was extremely intense. Endless columns of enemy aircraft bombed the city. The city was burning; for many kilometers the thick smoke overshadowed the sun." Soviet losses in the summer air battles at Stalingrad had been heavy. The arrival of the women aviators was to the rampant skepticism of the war-weary male pilots based near the city.

Pasportnikova: "Several of them did not want to fly in the same group as the women on combat missions. It was even more difficult for us, the mechanics; they could not accept us at all."

For Litvyak, who was small, blonde, and extremely attractive, the challenge of gaining the respect and acceptance of the male pilots on the ground was enormous, to say the least. In the air, however, it was a different matter. Inna Pasportnikova remembered that third day on the job for Litvyak: "Lilya was the wingman to the regimental commander. They spotted three Junkers 88s to the side of a bigger group of bombers. The leader decided to attack; Lilya followed his lead. She attacked so energetically that the bombers scattered and dropped their bombs. Taking advantage of this, her leader shot down one Ju-88 while Lilya killed a second." Then Litvyak

noticed her friend, Raya Belyaeva, chasing a Bf 109. Belyaeva ran out of ammunition and Lilya came to her aid, downing the German who turned out to be a leading Luftwaffe ace. Her achievement that day was all the more remarkable in view of the indisputable numerical advantage of the enemy aircraft at Stalingrad.

With each aerial victory, Lilya returned to her airfield and briefly celebrated the achievement with a few victory rolls and low passes, to the annoyance of Nikolai Baranov, the regimental commander, who invariably criticized her for the practice until she mollified him with her post-mission combat report.

On August 1, 1943, having already flown three sorties over the southern front and downing a Messerschmitt Bf 109 on the third, Lilya's group of nine Yak-1s encountered a flight of thirty Junkers Ju-88 bombers escorted by eighteen fighters. While attacking the bombers, a pair of 109s bounced her from out of the sun. Her plane disappeared into cloud cover. That was the last sighting of her by her fellow pilots. Her friend, Inna Pasportnikova, believing that the only course was to somehow find Litvyak's remains, determined to do so if it took the rest of her life. In 1979, a crash site was discovered on a farm near Dmitrievka where locals recalled that a woman pilot had been buried there. The body was located and exhumed and doctors declared that it was that of a small woman with a head injury. That information, and the location of the crash site, led to the Ministry of Defense modifying Lilya's records from "missing without a trace" to "killed in action, 1 August 1943."

On May 5, 1990, Chairman Mikhail Gorbachev conferred the title Hero of the Soviet Union on Lilya Litvyak. In March 1943, Tamara Pamyatnikh

and Raya Surnachevskaya, members of the all-female Soviet 586th Fighter Aviation Regiment, were assigned as duty fighters to patrol the airspace over Kastornaya. The rest of their air regiment had been scrambled to repel an air raid against Liski.

Large formations of German bombers had been sent to attack installations near the Kastornaya railway junction and the nearby bridge across the Don River. The other fighters of the regiment quickly destroyed two German bombers and dispersed the remainder. The fighters returned to their base to learn that Pamyatnikh and Surnachevskaya were long overdue. A search was launched and the wreckage of a Yak fighter was spotted. There was no sign of life near the wreck, and no sign of the other missing fighter. The remaining members of the 586th were depressed by the apparent loss of two of their most experienced pilots.

Tamara Pamyatnikh described their mission that spring day: "We were going toward the assigned grid square at an altitude of 4,000 meters. I saw some black dots to the southeast. I thought they were birds, but no, they were flying too high and too evenly. I had orders to attack. I waggled my wings at Raya to say 'follow me' and flew toward them.

"The ground controller, Lieutenant Slovokhotova, heard me say 'I see the enemy aircraft!' The written report by our squadron commander, Captain Agniya Polyantseva, states that Raya added, 'There are a lot of them!' and that our chief of staff, Captain Aleksandra Makunina, ordered 'Attack!' But our communications soon broke down and we heard nothing. We also knew that the rest of the regiment was fighting in another area. We were alone, but the sun was behind us, so we could

A Soviet female aviator and her Polikarpov Po-2.

surprise them. I saw one large group of enemy bombers and, farther back, another group of heavy bombers. [It is believed that there were at least forty-two Junkers Ju-88s and Dornier Do-215s in the German formations.]

"We had an opportunity to break up the formation with a surprise attack—they might think there were more of us if we flew down at them boldly. We had to try to prevent the bomb drop. So we both went into a steep dive and opened fire at the bombers flying in the center of the group. We pulled up into a chandelle and saw two burning aircraft falling. The explosions went up from the ground. The bomber group scattered. Then we went toward the next group, which was approaching in tight formation.

"They were bristling with machine guns. We attacked from behind and from the sides. The enemy directed concentrated fire at us. I saw the machine guns and a gunner's head. I could even discern the features of his face. Suddenly, my aircraft shuddered and then sharply turned over and started falling. I tried to open the cockpit canopy, but a powerful force pressed me into the seat. I could not lift my arms, and the ground kept coming closer with each second. The canopy finally broke off with a crack. I undid my safety harness with difficulty, and got out. My right hand instinctively pulled the ripcord ring. I felt the jolt from the opening parachute, and in an instant my feet touched the ground. My aircraft was burning beside me. My neck and face were bloody. I looked up at the sky. The enemy had turned and was going in a westerly direction with Raya still attacking. We had saved the station!

"Raya saw my airplane burning and falling. She told me that she was in despair at losing me and became

so careless that she forgot all the air combat rules and fired point-blank into the nearest Junkers. It went down abruptly, covered with black smoke, but so close that her plane was damaged [by explosion or debris] and she had to make a forced landing. She belly-landed the crippled plane, and a funny thing happened. People came running toward her armed with pitchforks, sticks, and rifles, thinking she was the enemy. They were amazed when they saw Raya and her red star emblem.

"The regiment heard that we were safe the next day, and Captain Olga Yamshchikova came to get us. She flew us very low over the battle site and the station. The locomotives were busy pulling out the trains loaded with troops. It made us happy, although we were in pain.

"Our great leader, Marina Raskova, chose the most experienced pilots she could find. The first came from

military units. It was very difficult for a woman to be a military pilot. One had to enter as ground personnel and work up. Very few did. When Raskova was placed in command of the all-female air corps group and we were sent to Engels for training, we crammed a three-year course into a few months. The mechanics had to work in bad weather for long hours; the navigators studied all the time, and the pilots had to get in 500 hours. We were equipped with Yak-1s, Yak-7Bs and Yak-9s. Operations started over Saratov, then to Stalingrad for the great battle from September to November 1942, and after that came the air battle over Kastornaya in early 1943. We had many other missions and covered important centers from east and west. We made about 5,000 sorties, were in 125 air battles, damaged forty-two enemy planes and destroyed thirty-eight."

far left: Polina Gelman; left: Marina Raskova

YOU CAN'T WIN THEM ALL

A Messerschmitt Bf 109 shot down over England in 1940.

LITTLE WILLIE WAS THE NAME painted just below the left canopy rail of the Hawker Hurricane of RAF Pilot Officer Alan Geoffrey Page. Before the outbreak of World War II, Page joined the University Air Squadron of London University and completed his flying training at Cranwell. He was flying as a member of No 56 Squadron from Rochford on August 12, 1940, at the height of the Battle of Britain. In his fine book, *Tale of a Guinea Pig*, and his conversations with me, he vividly recalled the events of that summer day: "One moment the sky between me and the thirty Dornier 215s was clear; the next it was crisscrossed with streams of white tracer from cannon shells converging on our Hurricanes.

"The first bang came as a shock. For an instant, I couldn't believe I'd been hit. Two more bangs followed in quick succession, and as if by magic a gaping hole suddenly appeared in my starboard wing.

"Surprise quickly changed to fear, and as the instinct of self-preservation began to take over, the gas tank behind the engine blew up, and my cockpit became an inferno. Fear became blind terror, then agonized horror as the bare skin of my hands gripping the throttle and control column shrivelled up like burned parchment under the intensity of the blast-furnace temperature. Screaming at the top of my voice, I threw my head back to keep it away from the searing flames. Instinctively, the tortured right hand groped for the release pin securing the restraining Sutton harness.

"'Dear God, save me . . . save me, dear God,' I cried imploringly. Then, as suddenly as terror had overtaken me, it vanished with the knowledge that death was no longer to be feared. My fingers kept up their blind and bloody groping. Some large, mechanical, dark object disappeared between my legs, and cool, relieving air suddenly flowed across my burning face. I tumbled. Sky, sea, sky, over and over as a clearing brain issued instructions to outflung limbs. 'Pull the ripcord—right hand to the ripcord.' Watering eyes focused on an arm flung out in space with some strange, meaty object attached at its end.

"More tumbling—more sky and sea, but with a blue-clad arm forming a focal point in the foreground. 'Pull the ripcord, hand,' the brain again commanded. Slowly but obediently, the elbow bent and the hand came across the body to rest on the chromium ring, but bounced away quickly with the agony of contact.

"More tumbling, but at a slower rate now. The weight of the head was beginning to tell.

"Realizing that pain or no pain, the ripcord had to be pulled, the brain overcame the reaction of the raw nerve endings and forced the mutilated fingers to grasp the ring and pull firmly.

"It acted immediately. With a jerk the silken canopy billowed in the clear summer sky.

"Quickly I looked up to see if the dreaded flames had done their work, and it was with relief that I saw that the shining material was unburned. Another fear rapidly followed. I heard the murmur of fading engines and firing guns, but it was the sun glinting on two pairs of wings that struck a chill through my heart. Stories of pilots being machine-gunned as they parachuted came flashing through my mind, and again I prayed for salvation. The two fighters straightened out and revealed themselves to be Hurricanes before turning away to continue the chase.

"It was then that I noticed the smell. The odor of my burned flesh was so loathsome that I wanted to vomit. But there was too much to attend to even for that small luxury.

"Self-preservation was my first concern, and my chance for it looked slim. The coastline at Margate was just discernible six to ten miles away; 10,000 feet below me lay the deserted sea. Not a ship or a seagull crossed the blank, gray surface.

"Still looking down I began to laugh. The force of the exploding gas tank had blown every vestige of clothing off from my thighs downwards, including one shoe. Carefully, I eased off the remaining shoe with the toes of the other foot and watched the tumbling footwear in the hope of seeing it strike the water far beneath. Now came the bad time.

"The shock of my violent injuries was starting to take hold, and this, combined with the cold air at the high altitude, brought on a shivering attack that was quite uncomfortable. With that, the parachute began to sway, setting up a violent oscillating movement with my torso acting as a human pendulum. Besides its swinging movement it began a gentle turn, and shortly afterwards the friendly shoreline disappeared behind my back. This brought with it an *idee fixe* that, if survival were to be achieved, then the coast must be kept in sight. A combination of agonized curses and bleeding hands pulling on the shrouds finally brought about the desired effect, and I settled back to the pleasures of closing eyes and burned flesh.

"Looking down again I was surprised to find that the water had come up to meet me very rapidly since last I had taken stock of the situation. This called for some fairly swift action if the parachute were to be discarded a second or two before entering the water. The procedure itself was quite simple. Lying over my stomach was a small, metal release box that clasped the four ends of the parachute harness after they had passed down over the shoulders and up from the groin. On this box was a circular metal disc that had to be turned through ninety degrees, banged, and presto, the occupant was released from the chute. All of this was extremely simple except in the case of fingers that refused to turn the little disc.

"The struggle was still in progress when I plunged feet first into the water. Despite the beauties of the summer and the wealth of warm days that had occurred, the sea felt icy cold to my badly shocked body. Kicking madly, I came to the surface to find my arms entangled with the multiple shrouds holding me in an octopus-like grip. The battle with the metal disc still had to be won, or else the water-logged parachute would eventually drag me down to a watery grave. Spluttering with mouthfuls of salt water, I struggled grimly with the vital release mechanism. Pieces of flesh flaked off and blood poured from the raw tissues.

"Desperation, egged on by near panic, forced the decision, and with a sob of relief I found that the disc had surrendered the battle.

"Kicking away blindly at the tentacles that still entwined arms and legs, I fought free and swam fiercely away from the nightmare surroundings of the parachute. Wild fear died away and the simple rules of procedure for continued existence exerted themselves again. 'Get rid of the chute, and then inflate your Mae West, and float about until rescued.'

"'That's all very well,' I thought, 'but unless I get near to the coast under my own steam, there's not much chance of being picked up.' With that I trod water and extricated the long rubber tube with which to blow up the jacket. Unscrewing the valves between my teeth, I searched my panting lungs for extra air. The only result after several minutes of exertion was a feeling of dizzyness and a string of bubbles from the bottom of the jacket. The fire had burned a large hole through the rubber bladder.

"Dismay was soon replaced by fatalism. There was the distant shore, unseen, but positioned by reference to the sun, and only one method of getting there, so it appeared. Turning on my stomach, I set out at a measured stroke. Ten minutes of acute misery passed by as the salt dried about my face injuries and the contracting strap of the flying helmet cut into the raw surface of my chin. Buckle and leather had welded into one solid mass, preventing removal of the headgear.

"Dumb despair then suddenly gave way to shining hope. The brandy flask, of course. This was it—the emergency for which it was kept. But the problem of undoing the tunic remained, not to mention that the tight-fitting Mae West covered the pocket as another formidable barrier. Hope and joy running too high to be deterred by such mundane problems, and so, turning with my face to the sky, I set about the task of getting slightly tipsy on neat brandy. Inch by inch my ultra-sensitive fingers worked their way under the Mae West toward the breast pocket. Every movement brought with it indescribable agony, but the goal was too great to allow for weakness. At last the restraining copper button was reached—a deep breath to cope with the pain—and it was undone. Automatically my legs kept up their propulsive efforts while my hand had a rest from its labors. Then, gingerly, the flask was eased out of its home and brought to the surface of the

Residents of Ponder's End with the remains of a Bf 110 shot down there on August 30, 1940.

A still from the 1941 film *I Wanted Wings* starring Ray Milland, William Holden, and Veronica Lake.

water. Pain became conqueror for a while and the flask was transferred to a position between my wrists. Placing the screw stopper between my teeth, I undid it with a series of head twists and finally the great moment arrived— the life-warming liquid was waiting to be drunk. Raising it to my mouth, I pursed my lips to drink. The flask slipped from between my wet wrists and disappeared from sight. Genuine tears of rage followed this newest form of torture, which in turn gave place to a furious determination to swim to safety.

"After the first few angry strokes despair returned in full force, ably assisted by growing fatigue, cold, and pain. Time went by unregistered. Was it minutes, hours, or days since my flaming Hurricane disappeared between my legs? Was it getting dark or were my eyes closing up? How could I steer toward the shore if I couldn't see the sun? How could I see the sun if that rising pall of smoke obscured it from sight?

"That rising pall of smoke . . . that rising pall of smoke. No, it couldn't be. I yelled, I splashed the water with my arms and legs until the pain brought me to a sobbing halt. Yes, the smoke was coming from a funnel—but supposing it passed without seeing me? Agony of mind was greater than agony of body and the shouting and splashing recommenced. Looking again, almost expecting that smoke and funnel had been a hallucination, I gave a fervent gasp of thanks to see that, whatever ship it was, it had hove to.

"All of the problems were fast disappearing and only one remained. It was one of keeping afloat for just another minute or two before all energy failed. Then I heard it—the unmistakable chug-chug of a small motorboat growing steadily louder.

Soon it came into sight with a small bow pouring away to each side. In it sat two men in the strange garb peculiar to sailors of the British Merchant Service. The high-revving note of the engine died to a steady throb as the man astride the engine throttled back. Slowly the boat circled without attempting to pick me up. A rough voice carried over the intervening water. 'What are you? A Jerry or one of ours?'

"My weak reply was gagged by a mouthful of water. The other man tried as the boat came full circle for the second time. 'Are you a Jerry, mate?'

"Anger flooded through me. Anger, not at these sailors who had every reason to let a German pilot drown, but anger at the steady chain of events since the explosion that had reduced my tortured mind and body to its present state of near-collapse. And anger brought with it temporary energy. 'You stupid pair of fucking bastards, pull me out!'

"The boat altered course and drew alongside. Strong arms leaned down and dragged my limp body over the side and into the bottom of the boat. 'The minute you swore, mate,' one of them explained, 'we knew you was an RAF officer.'

"The sodden, dripping bundle was deposited on a wooden seat athwart ships. A voice mumbled from an almost lifeless body as the charred helmet was removed. One of the sailors leaned down to catch the words. 'What did you say, chum?' 'Take me to the side. I want to be sick.'

"The other man answered in a friendly voice, 'You do it in the bottom of the boat, and we'll clean it up afterwards.'

"But habit died hard and pride wouldn't permit it, so, keeping my head down between my knees, I was

able to control the sensation of nausea. Allowing me a moment or two to feel better, the first sailor produced a large knife. 'Better get this wet stuff off you, mate. You don't want to catch your death of cold.'

"The absurdity of death from a chill struck me as funny and I chuckled for the first time in a long while. To prove the sailor's point, the teeth chattering recommenced. Without further ado the man with the knife set

to work and deftly removed pieces of my life jacket and tunic with the skill of a surgeon. Then my naked body was wrapped up in a blanket produced from the seat locker.

"One of them went forward to the engine and seconds later the little boat was churning her way back to the mother ship. The other sailor sat down beside me in silence, anxious to help but not knowing what to do next. I sensed the kindness of his atti-

tude and felt that it was up to me to somehow offer him a lead. The feeling of sickness was still there from the revolting smell of burned flesh, but I managed to gulp out, 'Been a lovely . . . summer, hasn't it?'"

"One bright morning I was standing on the edge of the airfield when two white Very lights [the signal for 'Scramble!'] hurtled skywards. I automatically turned to look at the

below: Major Winslow "Mike" Sobanski, 4FG, was killed on D-Day when his fighter was shot down over northern France; left: Lieutenant Ralph "Kid" Hofer was killed on July 2, 1944 when his Mustang was shot down by Bf 109s over Budapest. He was also a member of the famous 4FG.

Readiness Typhoons, their engines always warm so they would soon be away. I was surprised to see no 'Tiffies' in their usual spot at the end of the East-West runway, but a loud roaring of engines from the direction of 257 dispersal signified action somewhere. Quickly, two Typhoons were tearing across the grass using a short runway, more or less West-East. Caught with their pants down, the two pilots were 'scrambling' down-wind, in echelon port formation, and not seeing a small Royal Navy aircraft approaching to land from the other direction. Too late, the control tower banged off a red warning signal and the next seconds were mayhem. The leading Typhoon, attempting to avoid the incoming aircraft, lifted off early and tried to turn to starboard and towards me. Without enough flying speed for such a maneuver the right wing stalled, hit the ground, and the Typhoon cartwheeled over and over again. I started to run toward the tumbling aircraft as I saw the pilot thrown clear and tossed like a cork a hundred feet into the air. I was running so fast that the pilot hit the ground seconds before I reached him. His safety straps had broken and in his parachute harness he lay in a crumpled heap, bloody and broken in every limb. I knelt down, drew my sheath knife from my flying boot, and

started to cut into the harness. His lips moved and his limbs twitched. I was horrified, but I had to do something. Bits of aircraft strewn about were smouldering and I felt so inadequate. I was grateful when the ambulance arrived and relieved me of the responsibility. My good friend, Flight Lieutenant Dusty Miller, mercifully died before arriving in hospital."
—Pilot Officer Nick Berryman, formerly with No 276 Squadron, RAF

"We took our losses. My best friend . . . I lost him. I went down to the flight line till the sun was down, still in hope he would get in there. He didn't make it. But you accept it. The old crutch . . . it's gonna happen to somebody else; it's not gonng happen to me. This is a great piece of faith. You're wrong! But this is what you believe."
—Captain William O'Brien, USAF (Ret), formerly with the 357th Fighter Group, Eighth USAAF

Hornchurch airfield was home on August 31, 1940 to No 54 Squadron, RAF, and to Spitfire pilot Al Deere: "The morning was strangely and ominously quiet in the Hornchurch Sector, particularly in view of the good weather, and it was not until about mid-day that the squadron received the order to scramble. We had just taxied into position for takeoff and were all lined up ready to go, when a counter order was passed over the R/T. No sooner were we again parked in dispersal with engines stopped than a wildly gesticulating telephone orderly indicated that we were to start up again. In a matter of seconds all twelve aircraft were again taxiing to the takeoff end, urged on by the controller's now near-hysterical voice shouting over the R/T, 'Hornet aircraft, get airborne as quickly as you can; enemy in the immediate vicinity.'

"Hurriedly, desperately, for I had no wish to be caught taking off, I swung my aircraft into wind to find my takeoff run blocked by a Spitfire, the pilot of which was looking vaguely around for his position in the formation. 'Get to hell out of the way, Red Two,' I bellowed, recognizing my number two from the letters on his aircraft. It was a second or two before he made up his mind to move; immediately he did so, I opened the throttle and careered across the airfield in pursuit of the squadron, which had, by now, cleared the far hedge and, with wheels retracting, was turning and climbing away from the airfield.

"I was not quite airborne when a bomb burst on the airfield ahead of me and to my left. 'Good, I've made it,' I thought. To this day I'm not clear exactly what happened next; all I can remember is that a tremendous blast of air, carrying showers of earth, struck me in the face, and that the next moment I was thinking vaguely that I was upside down, still firmly strapped in the cockpit. Stones and dirt were thrown into my face and my helmet was torn by the stony ground against which my head was firmly pressed.

"Finally the aircraft stopped its mad, upside-down dash, leaving me trapped in the cockpit, in almost total darkness and breathing petrol fumes, the smell of which was overpowering. Bombs were still exploding outside, but this was not as frightening as the thought of fire from the petrol now seeping into the ground around my head. One spark and I would have been engulfed in flames."

General Lieutnant a.D. Günther Rall, German air force (Ret), recalled a day in May 1944 during the defense of the Reich: "After nearly three years in Russia, my last action was at Cape

Chersones, to the west of Sebastopol. Here combat troops concentrated in the Crimean Peninsula and defended eight kilometers of land, before the chaos of the retreat over 400 kilometers of open sea to Romania began. Here the order came by radio for my reassignment as commander of the II/JG to the defense forces of the Reich. I left Russia with mixed feelings.

"Twelfth May 1944. Five a.m. Telephone call from the division commander—listening in on the enemy radio communications—we are expecting mammoth air strikes by the Eighth U.S. Air Force. In reaction to this, two big air defense squadrons were readied—altogether fifty Fw 190s. My group of twenty-five Me 109Gs as top cover against the long-range fighter escorts. Takeoff when U.S. advance fighters are over the Zuider Zee. Rendezvous with our own heavy groups over Steinhudern Sea. En route climb up to 8,000 meters, my group 3,000 meters overhead. The contrails come in sight—we climb higher (no pressurization, no air conditioning in the cockpit). We are above the contrails—about 11,000 meters high. Order: Battle Formation! Orders to me from the 7th Air Division. Take over the whole formation, no radio communication exists to the formation leader of the heavy groups. At 8,000 metres I make contact with a P-47 formation and attack with my group. I come within firing range of the leading element, a P-47 in my sight. I fire—a huge flame and explosion, the P-47 goes down, the second follows after a short fire exchange—the leader goes down after hectic defensive maneuvers. At this moment I am being attacked from above and behind me by the second element (four P-47s). My wingman announces engine failure and bails out. Now I am being hunted by four

P-47s who are flying in line abreast behind me, and are within firing range. Against all rules, I crash dive, although I know that the Thunderbolts are faster in the dive and structurally stable—but I have no other option. While diving, the first hits burst into my Me 109, into the body, engine, radiator, and suddenly a hit and an explosion—the thumb of my left hand is shot away while holding the throttle. My windshield ices up. I cannot see how high up I am. I clutch the stick between my legs and scrape the ice from the windshield with my still usable hand. At treetop level I pull up my Me 109 so steeply, it reaches the stalling point. The machine is on its back. I blow off the cockpit roof and try to jump out—difficult—the force from the upside-down plane pushes me into the cockpit. Instinctively, my reflex movements come into play and I manage to free myself. I begin tumbling, and it is impossible to reach my parachute handle. After a seemingly endless free fall, I stabilize myself . . . I finally reach the handle, I pull it and the parachute opens! What a feeling! But now the pain from the wound of the missing thumb hits me. I glide about another 500 meters into a forest and I get hung up on trees. Thank God for that. It could have been very dangerous to land on my back after a previous injury involving three broken vertebrae. The danger is not over. After the quick release from the parachute, I tumble head-over-heels into a ravine—but I survived—and somehow I feel lucky.

"Many years later an air force historian identified my opponents as Hub Zemke's Wolf Pack. My group suffered heavy losses in this action. We always fought against heavy odds, always realizing the certainty that every second pilot wasn't coming back. Why did we keep on fighting?

Vapor trails of an air battle over Lewes captured by photographer Edward Reeves during the Battle of Britain.

Colonel Francis Gabreski had over fifteen years in operational and command duties in WWII, the Korean War, and after. In the European theater he flew with the 56FG, Hub Zemke's Wolf Pack, from Boxted and Halesworth.

Nobody believed in victory anymore. It was simply the unwritten law . . . to save what could be saved and keep the German cities from destruction. In the end, no one thought even that was going to happen.

"Later on, I became good friends with Hub Zemke. We understood each other."

"I remember seeing a new pilot on his first mission crash on takeoff and burst into flames after turning over and skidding through a fence. I flew right over the black smoke coming from the wreckage as I took off and thought, 'What a pity, a nice young man of nineteen on this first mission.' Our group flight surgeon was always at the end of the runway in his jeep, which was loaded with all kinds of emergency equipment, axe, hatchet, fire extinguisher, medical supplies, etc. He rushed to the burning plane, knocked out the canopy, dug down into the ground, and pulled the dazed pilot from the wreckage, then dragged him away from the plane, which shortly afterwards blew up. He got the Soldier's Medal for his heroism.

"When I got back from the mission, I reported to Squadron Intelligence for debriefing and, much to my shock and amazement, there stood this young fighter pilot, grinning from ear to ear, and saying, 'How did it go today, fellas?' I nearly fell over. What a happy ending to a tragic accident. He suffered only a small cut on the little finger of his left hand."
—Colonel Bert McDowell, Jr, USAF (Ret), formerly with the 55th Fighter Group, Eighth USAAF

"I had lined up behind an Me 109 over France, while flying a Spitfire. I had the enemy aircraft in the center of my gunsight and I was ready to press my thumb on the firing button . . . but to

no avail. I was dumbfounded and furious. I couldn't press the firing button. My thumb was frozen.

"That was a lesson in defeat for me because I lost a positive kill.

"I never did like to fly with gloves on my hands during the war, so I paid for it that day. However, our flight surgeon did all he could to revive my frostbitten thumb.

"The doc directed that I use my gloves whenever I flew after that, and I did. But when I arrived at the combat zone, I had to take the gloves off because they made me feel uncomfortable. Of course, on the way back to our airfield in England, I put them on again . . . just in case the flight surgeon should be at the dispersal waiting to check on me."
—Colonel Steve Pisanos, USAF (Ret), formerly with the 4th Fighter Group, Eighth USAAF

A midair collision can ruin one's day. For 1st Lieutenant Paul Riley of the 4th Fighter Group, that day was April 24, 1944. It began inauspiciously when Riley's P-51B Mustang shed its right wing drop tank on takeoff, forcing him to abort the mission. He quickly told his wingman to take over his position, and continued down the Debden runway to his revetment where his wing tank was replaced and the new tank filled. In ten minutes he was airborne and, by pushing the fighter hard, was able to catch up with his squadron.

The Mustangs were climbing to 25,000 feet when his CO reported up to eighteen Fw 190s slightly below and directly ahead of the American formation. Riley focused on two Fws ahead of him and rapidly closed on one, firing a four-second burst into the German machine. The Focke Wulf nosed over and started lazily down. Riley looked around and, seeing no friendly aircraft, decided to follow

his "kill" down from their 18,000-foot altitude to confirm the crash on gun-camera film. For a confirmed credit, a pilot needed either witnesses to the downing, or combat film of the enemy plane on fire, crashing, or of the enemy pilot bailing out.

On the way down Riley saw tracers passing over his left wing and quickly pulled up hard and to the left. Almost immediately his left wing collided with another Fw 190 and the propeller of the enemy fighter sliced off about twenty-five percent of the wing, causing the Mustang to tumble end over end. In the collision, the lieutenant's left leg was broken.

Dazed, but recovering from the shock of what had just happened, Riley managed to keep the Mustang flying by using full power, and tried to set a course westward toward France. Soon, though, he encountered some flak and his plane was hit, setting his left wing on fire. He prepared to bail out but, in his haste to leave the burning aircraft, he neglected to disconnect his radio-telephone plug and found himself caught halfway in and out of the cockpit.

Finally freed of the R/T connection, he was falling through space, where he pulled the D-ring of his parachute and found that he was only taking up slack in the cable. Struggling now at low altitude, he at last felt his shoulders yanked backward and almost instantly impacted on the soft, dark earth of a newly-plowed German potato field.

He crawled through the furrows, dragging his badly injured leg, and noticed that his Mustang had crashed just to the rear of a German passenger train. At that moment, the flak crew that had shot him down arrived and one of them, a young kid, greeted Riley with the traditional "For you the war is over." Paul Riley spent the next

My Goodness — My GUINNESS

thirteen months in a German prisoner of war camp.

"In the evening of Sunday, March 11, 1945, the U.S. Navy aircraft carrier *Randolf*, anchored in the Ulithi Lagoon, was hit by a Japanese kamikaze [suicide plane] twin-engined Frances bomber, blowing a huge hole in the starboard quarter of the ship and putting her out of action for nearly a month. I was working in our squadron office just beneath the flight deck and about 250 feet from where the kamikaze hit. When the tremendous explosion occurred, the shock bounced us out of our chairs. I ran up to the flight deck and saw the entire aft end of the carrier ablaze with huge clouds of black smoke boiling up. I then went down to the hangar deck where the aft end was also blazing. There were bodies about the deck, some badly mangled. I went forward to the bow to get away from the fire and smoke. The ship's firefighters were able to get the blaze under control in a remarkably short time, but the extent of the damage was staggering. A 40 × 40 × 40–foot section of the starboard quarter was missing from just below the hangar deck on up through the flight deck, and the flight deck area around the hole was twisted upwards. Soon, a repair ship, the *Jason*, came alongside and in about three weeks the *Randolf* was repaired."

—Commander Hamilton McWhorter, U.S. Navy (Ret), formerly with VF-12

Shot down over France, Captain Jack Ilfrey was assisted by French civilians to successfully evade capture by the Germans, cycling 150 miles to the Allied lines on the coast. In two tours, he completed 142 missions.

August 27, 1940 was an exciting day for residents of Tavistock when a Dornier Do-17 was shot down near their town.

AIR FIGHTER

On April 11, 1944, Lieutenant Mark Stapleton and fellow pilots of the 357FG were engaged in a savage dogfight over Leipzig, Germany: "My guns jammed after each short burst, but thanks to an experimental hydraulic gun charger that had been installed in my plane, I was able to clear the jam and fire again. My guns jammed and were cleared at least seven times. I overran the enemy aircraft at which time Lieutenant Sumner closed and observed hits on the enemy aircraft, which crashed and exploded."

"It's just like being in a knife fight in a dirt-floor bar. If you want to fix a fella, the best way to do it is to get behind him and stick him in the back. It's the same in an air fight. If you want to kill that guy, the best thing to do is get around behind him where he can't see you . . . and shoot him."
—Captain William O'Brien, formerly with the 357th Fighter Group, Eighth USAAF

"There are two things a fighter pilot must have to do his work in combat, and that he can't really acquire anywhere else except in combat: Confidence in his ability to kill, and confidence in his ability to get away when in trouble.

"If you feel you can kill and feel they can't kill you, then you'll have the offensive spirit. Without that offensive spirit—the ability to lunge instantaneously and automatically like a fighting cock at the enemy the moment you spot him—you are lost. You either 'go along for the ride' as we call it when a fella hangs back and doesn't make kills, or eventually you get shot down.

"I know, because it took me quite a long time to build up confidence in myself, which I had thought I had when I left home, and there was quite a long time when I went along just for the ride."
—Major Don Gentile, formerly with the 4th Fighter Group, Eighth USAAF

"To be a good fighter pilot, there is one prime requisite—think fast and act faster."
—Major John T. Godfrey, formerly with the 4th Fighter Group, Eighth USAAF

"I think that the most important features of a fighter pilot are aggressiveness and professionalism. They are both needed to achieve the fighter

Major Hank Mills of the 334FS, 4FG, at Debden, England, in 1943.

pilot's goal: the highest score within the shortest time, with the least risk to himself and his wingman."
—Colonel Gidi Livni, formerly and F-16 pilot with the Israeli Air Force

"An air victory certainly gave you a great satisfaction. You, as a pilot, saw primarily the airplane as your target and not so much its pilot. Only when you got a chance to see the debris and the dead pilot on the ground did you get a mixed feeling and sympathy. We, the German fighter pilots, saw many losses of our own in the air. I, personally, was shot down eight times, three of them with serious injuries, but we had to fly again."
—Generalleutnant a.D. Günther Rall, German air force (Ret)

"I am not an ace. I believe I am credited with three and a half victories. I had many inconclusive dogfights. When in a dogfight, one is giving it 150 percent attention. You are pulling G and trying to look behind you with your neck on a swivel (why do you suppose fighter pilots wear scarves?). So often, on both sides, aircraft were shot down without the pilots knowing what hit them. On one occasion our squadron over the Netherlands was bounced; one section didn't get the message to break and three Spitfires went down with no defensive action whatever. At the same time, we would often see enemy aircraft below. The CO and his section would dive down and knock down two or three before the enemy aircraft realized they were being attacked.

"Most pilots wanted to stay on operations. It was a feeling you got on a good squadron—a sense of being one with your fellow pilots and a determination to do your utmost to deserve their respect and friendship. I firmly believe that pilots often flew

when their medical condition should have required treatment, but they did not want to let the squadron down.

"Every pilot, or serviceman, no doubt has their own way of dealing with fear. For my brother and me the waiting after briefing was the most worrisome time. You knew that there was a certain element of danger involved, and you could think about it. However, once you started your engine and began to taxi you were so busy taking care of what you had to do that you didn't think about the danger. In the air you had so much going on that required your attention and action, there was no time to be afraid."
—Flight Lieutenant Douglas Warren, RCAF (Ret), formerly with Nos 66 and 165 Squadrons, RAF

"The squadron was doing well in Huns. [Captain Albert] Ball came back every day with a bag of one or more. Besides his SE 5, he had a Nieuport Scout, the machine in which he had done so well the previous year. He had a roving commission, and, with two machines, was four hours a day in the air. Of the great fighting pilots his tactics were the least cunning. Absolutely fearless, the odds made no difference to him. He would always attack, single out his man, and close. On several occasions he almost rammed the enemy, and often came back with his machine shot to pieces.

"One morning, before the rest of us had gone out on patrol, we saw him coming in rather clumsily to land. He was not a stunt pilot, but flew very safely and accurately, so that, watching him, we could not understand his awkward, floating landing. But when he taxied up to the sheds we saw his elevators were flapping loose—controls had been completely shot away. He had flown back from the lines and made his landing entirely by winding his adjustable tail up and down! It was incredible he had not crashed. His oil tank had been riddled, and his face and the whole nose of the machine were running with black castor oil. He was so angry at being shot up like this that he walked straight to the sheds, wiped oil off his shoulders and face with a rag, ordered out his Nieuport and within two hours was back with yet another Hun to his credit!

"Ball was a quiet, simple little man. His one relaxation was the violin, and his favourite after dinner amusement to light a red magnesium flare outside his hut and walk round it in his pyjamas fiddling! He was meticulous in the air of his machines, guns, and in the examination of his ammunition. He never flew for amusement. The only trips he took, apart from offensive patrols, were the minimum requisite to test his engines or fire at the ground target [when] sighting his guns. He never boasted or criticized, but his example was tremendous."
—from *Sagittarius Rising* by Cecil Lewis, formerly with No 56 Squadron, RFC

General Johannes Steinhoff, formerly with JGVII, German air force: "I have always wondered whether it was man's aggressive disposition to hunt that triggered one's reflexes so swiftly and immediately or whether it was the experience gained in a hundred dogfights that prompted one to make the right decisions in a fraction of a second—whether in defense or in attack. Undoubtedly, the state of extreme tension was partly responsible for that reflex reaction, as well as the fact that years of practice at sneaking up on the enemy, dodging out of his way, and hiding in the infinity of the sky had developed new and unknown instincts in the few who had survived."

"I think the most significant properties of a good combat fighter pilot are attitude and opportunity. He must have a desire to close with the enemy and destroy him, and he must possess or create the chance to engage his opponent. All the other components—marksmanship, eyesight, airmanship, etc.—will flow from attitude and opportunity."
—Captain William O'Brien, USAF (Ret), formerly with the 357th Fighter Group, Eighth USAAF

Major Jonathan Holdaway, USAF, was an exchange officer with the RAF on No 43 Squadron, flying F3 Tornado aircraft from RAF Leuchars in Scotland: "The exchange is normally about a three-year tour. I extended for six months. I leave this summer [1998] to go back to the States. We have exchanges with numerous air forces around the world. It's a two-year tour following completion of whatever training those nations put us through. When pilots or aircrew come over to the UK on exchange with the RAF, we go through ten to twelve months of training before they send us to whatever squadron we will be assigned to, and then, once you show up on the squadron, it's normally for two years. I actually started out flying the Hawk at Valley, Wales, which is a trainer. They do that because the flying system and the rules and regulations that the RAF have are quite different from the USAF, so they put us through a short course in the Hawk that lasts about three months, purely to familiarize us with the way the airspace regulations are set up here in the UK—to get us used to their way of doing business. Then they send us to whatever training course we're going to go through. For me, it was the Tornado F3. We

Luftwaffe pilots with their Messerschmitt Bf 109 fighters in France.

have other guys on the Tornado GR1, the Jaguar, some guys on the Harrier, some on C-130s. There's generally at least one exchange officer in each type of plane the RAF flies."

"I sort of divided luck, or pilotage I guess you'd say, into several categories. The first thing you've got to do is get an airplane and make sure it's ready to go. If you're very careful about that, you eliminate an awful lot of the bad luck. But you could still use good luck. Every once in a while a part would break or something . . . while you were flying. I always used to know where I was going to land in case of an emergency. You're always picking out places to land. So, if you had it happen in the air, and you had any control over the plane, the luck [requirement] was cut down, way down . . . but you could always use a little.

"When you're in combat, if you trained properly and planned your missions properly, you could eliminate a lot of the luck requirement. If a pilot said that luck was worth maybe 50 percent of your survival overall, I'd say that, by doing those things, you'd cut it down to maybe 10 percent. I didn't drink in those days. I didn't run around to the pubs with the guys on the time off. I always did my studying of airplanes, targets, and how to attack them. I never lost a guy that flew with me on a mission. We always planned the mission properly, as well as we could. I went out and spent a lot of time attacking English gun posts, gun emplacements, going over and visiting with people and becoming familiar with their weapons, and I soon found out where they had blank spaces on their predictors, and all the rest of it. So, all I needed was intelligence reconnaissance pictures of a given airfield, for instance, or a town or whatever—

wherever they had emplacements—and I could look at 'em and tell you where you could attack them without getting shot at. That's where I did the attacking, and the hell with getting shot at when you didn't have to. And there were little things—things you could do—if you did them that way all the time, you had a good chance of not getting shot down. So, I would say that part of it was hard work, nose-to-the-grindstone kind of thing, and planning, and a lot of practice.

"I had good eyesight and I was serious. I'd been flyin' longer than most . . . had more hours than most. I certainly did more missions than anybody else. I figured things out when they weren't figuring them out, and I never did just blindly follow somebody's plan that they'd figured out. I always figured out a mission myself even when I wasn't leading. It's using your head, all your faculties . . . and flying ability, too. I'm not saying I was the best ever. You've got to have a knack about you, about doing the right thing at the right time . . . making decisions when you know damn well everything else is wrong, or sounds wrong anyway, and you've got to have the guts not only to make the decision, but to do it."
—Major General Carroll W. McColpin, USAF (Ret)

Japanese ace Saburo Sakai and eight of his fellow Imperial Navy pilots of the Tainan Wing flew their Zero fighters from Rabaul, to their new field at Lae, New Guinea, on April 8, 1942. They had been told that the move was in preparation for the complete occupation of New Guinea by Japanese forces. At Lae they found a tiny runway not more than 3,000 feet long, no control tower, no hangars, and no maintenance facilities. The field was tightly enclosed by mountains

Ground crew personnel of the 56th Fighter Group relaxing near some of their P-47 Thunderbolt charges.

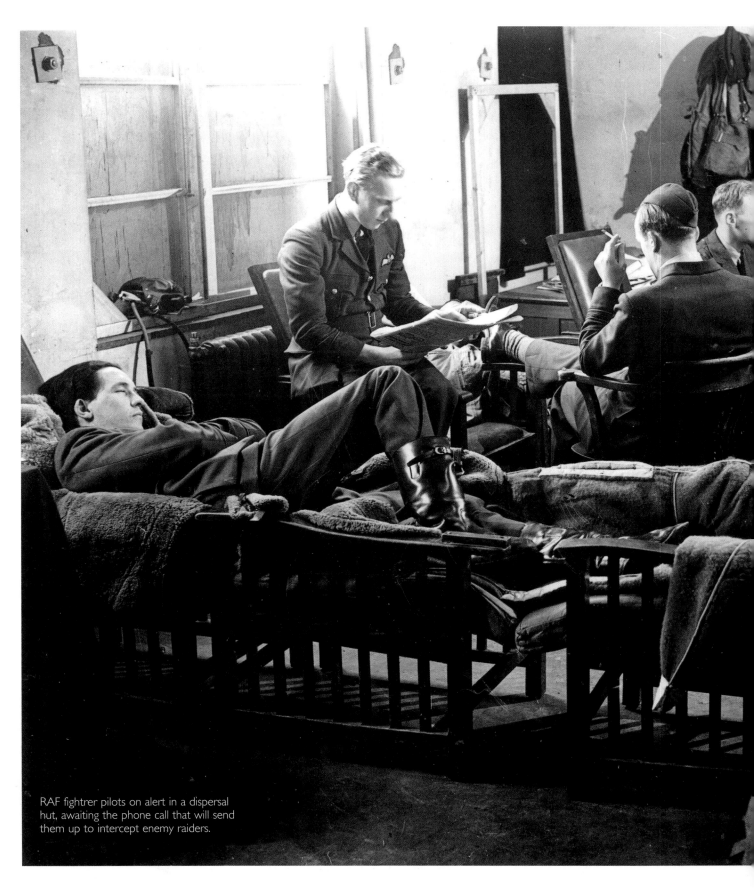

RAF fightrer pilots on alert in a dispersal hut, awaiting the phone call that will send them up to intercept enemy raiders.

on three sides and, as he began his approach, the prospect of operating from it made Sakai cringe. The arriving airmen were greeted by the other twenty-one pilots of the Wing, who had flown in several days earlier, and were given the grand tour.

In the next four months Sakai and the members of the new Lae Wing fell into a dull, unvarying routine. Mechanics began their labors at 2:30 each morning. The pilots were roused at 3:30 and took exactly the same breakfast—a dish of rice, soybean paste soup with dried vegetables and pickles—each day. Sakai recalled the fare at Lae as 'pitifully inadequate.'

With breakfast finished, an alert flight of six Zeros, whose engines had already been warmed up, sat primed for immediate takeoff to intercept any enemy aircraft in the area. The pilots waited by the fighters, which had been positioned by the end of the runway. They could be airborne in seconds.

The other pilots of the Wing tended to hang around the command post awaiting orders. They played chess and checkers to pass the time.

A patrol formation was launched every morning at eight. If a bomber escort effort was ordered, the Zeros flew a southeasterly course down the Papuan coast, joining with the bombers at Buna. The Lae pilots were normally back at the field by noon for the usual uninspired lunch of rice and canned fish or meat. Between meals, Sakai recalled, all the pilots were given fruit juice and candy to help make up for the vitamin deficiency of their diets.

The routine continued at five each evening with all pilots gathering for compulsory callisthenics, followed by supper, bathing, and letter-writing or reading. They were usually in bed by eight or nine.

At their Lae base there was little recreation or amusement, and there were no women. The only entertainment occurred when a few of the pilots produced a harmonica, guitar, or ukelele. Yet Sakai remembered that their morale was high and that there were few complaints. They were fighter pilots, there to engage the enemy in combat. They wanted to fight.

Peter Townsend was one of the most famous and highest-achieving fighter pilots of World War II. He recalled the day war broke out, September 3, 1939, when he was with No 43 Squadron at RAF Tangmere, Sussex: "At that moment on the grass at Tangmere airfield I was lying beside my Hurricane watching flaky white clouds drift across a blue sky, while hovering larks shrilled and voices came to me from pilots and ground crew also lying beside their dispersed aircraft. Never in my life had I experienced to so peaceful a scene.

"At eleven a.m. Squadron Adjutant John Simpson walked into the hangar and said to Warrant Officer Chitty, 'The balloon goes up at eleven-fifteen. That's official.'

"We all foregathered in the mess, where we had listened to Hitler's shrieking voice just a year ago. Our station commander, Fred Sowrey, looked grave. But the presence of this veteran was reassuring for us who did not know war. Twenty-three years earlier to the very day, Fred Sowery had been on patrol with Lieutenant Leefe Robinson when Robinson sent a Zeppelin crashing in flames near London. Then Zeppelin L32 had fallen to Sowery's guns, and in May 1918, he was in at the kill of the last German raider to crash on English soil. This veteran of the first generation of airmen was about to see the horror of a second attempt by the Germans to reduce England to her knees by

RAF Spitfire pilots between scrambles at Hawkinge.

The pilot of a Focke-Wulf Fw 190 preparing to fly in the defense of the Reich against Allied bombers.

bombing. He steadied us in our ardour to 'get at the Hun.' He told us, 'Don't think a fighter pilot's life is one of endless flying and glory. You will spend nine-tenths of your time sitting on your backsides waiting.'"

"The fighter pilot has extensive training; he is familiar with his airplane, he has confidence in his skills as a pilot, he has been briefed on all aspects of combat flying, he has camaraderie with his flight and squadron buddies, and he has the youth to embrace excitement and adventure. No fear—only that nagging thought that he can go down in flames, just as he has seen others go down, but he allows this thought only a fleeting moment in the certain knowledge that such things happen to other people, not to him.

"Consider personality and character. The quiet type who simply goes about his pilot job with skill and courage . . . the fighter who breaks rank and discipline to chase anything that moves in the air or on the ground, anything that will give him an excuse to pull the trigger . . . the cautious type who doesn't make a move in the air until he has assessed the situation . . . the aggressive type who seeks out the enemy, employing skill and a knowledge of his aircraft to bring maximum damage to the enemy—he is the most effective of them all . . . and finally, the apathetic type, who looks forward to completing his tour."
—Lieutenant Robert Strobell, formerly with the 353rd Fighter Group, Eighth USAAF

"The fighter pilots were another breed of cat. On their personal skill and aggressiveness depended not only their lives and the lives of their teammates, but the lives of the bomber crews and the success of the air war."
—Colonel Budd J. Peaslee, formerly with the 384th Bomb Group, Eighth USAAF

Bobby Richards was Johnny Godfrey's roommate at Debden. They had been friends for two years. On Saturday, March 4, 1944, Lieutenant Richards died when his P-51B Mustang crashed 800 yards southwest of Durban's Farm, near the small Suffolk town of Framlingham, England.

The 4th Fighter Group had very little experience with their new Mustangs, having transitioned to them from P-47s just a few days before the escort mission on which Richards was killed. The group had taken their Mustangs into combat just twice before March 4. In his excellent book, *The Look of Eagles,* Godfrey recalled: "Rumors had been flying hot and heavy that we were being transferred from P-47s to P-51s. We had heard a lot of talk about this amazing plane . . . it was capable of 1,800-mile flights with its two [wing] tanks. Our P-47s had only one belly tank which was slung underneath the fuselage. The 51s had them slung underneath each wing, with two more permanent tanks in the wing and another tank just to the rear of the cockpit.

"On February 22, the rumors became a fact; one P-51 landed and we were all (sixty pilots) ordered to fly it in preparation for the change-over. It was a beautiful airplane; it reminded me of the Spitfire with its huge in-line engine. And, like the Spitfire, it, too, was glycol-cooled. We queued up on the plane like housewives at a bargain sale. The time in the air was spread very thin, forty minutes was all the time I had in the air in a '51 when, on the morning of the 28th the group flew to Steeple Morden Base in their P-47s and traded them for P-51s. The planes didn't have their auxiliary tanks on, but they

Major Louis "Red Dog" Norley of the 4FG was among the first American fighter pilots over Berlin; right: Credited with 14 1/2 victories, Major Howard "Deacon" Hively also flew with the 4FG at Debden.

were full of fuel and the machine guns were loaded. Our briefing was held on the ground among our '51s. No flying back to Debden for us, but off on a fighter sweep to France. We were familiarizing ourselves with this plane the hard way.

"The Air Force had made no mistake when they made their purchase of Mustangs from North American Aviation. They were the hottest planes in the skies. From zero to 30,000 feet they were able to match anything the Luftwaffe put into the air. If the fighting spirit of the group was high before the advent of the '51, it was now at a fever pitch.

"But horrible little bugs were plaguing the '51s—motor trouble, gas trouble, radio trouble—and the worst bug of all, besides our windows frosting up, was in our machine guns. At high altitudes they froze up on us; moreover, in a dogfight they were often jammed by the force of gravity in a turn. That meant straightening out before firing, a feat that was practically impossible under the circumstances. Technicians were rushed to the base to iron out our problems. The war was still going on and the great air offensive against Germany was now in full swing, so we had to fly them, bugs and all . . .

"[On March 4] Bob was flying on my wing over the Channel. He called me, 'Hello, Shirt Blue Red Leader, this is Red Two. My motor's acting up, am returning to base.'

"'Roger, Red Two.' I didn't know it then, but those were the last words I was to hear from Bob. Motor difficulty was common in those days, and over the radio I could hear other boys reporting trouble. On approaching the Dutch coast my own engine started coughing and spitting. It was my turn now.

"Of the sixteen planes that took off that morning, only three from our squadron were able to meet the

Mustang pilots returning from an escort mission in 1944.

bombers over Berlin. Those three returned safely to the base. The three missing boys were from the other two squadrons. Weather was very bad over England. I started to let down through the clouds, but when ice formed on my wings, I turned back toward the Channel.

"Emerging from the clouds I flew south, letting down gradually until 500 feet above the Channel, then I turned back to England and flew at 600 feet just below the cloud base.

"Bob was not at Debden when I landed, but I didn't worry, and in fact gave no thought to it even an hour later when I still had no word. Probably he had landed at Martlesham Heath to see J.J. (our buddy, Joseph Jack), and just forgot to call the base. I was still sitting in the dispersal hut when the phone in the intelligence room rang. I heard low talking but the words were indistinct. Mac, the intelligence officer, approached me with a bottle and a glass. At the end of every mission a glass of whiskey was always given to the pilot, if he wished, to settle his nerves.

Bob's plane crashed at Framlingham. He was still in the cockpit. He's dead, Johnny.'

"His words hit me like a lightning bolt. It just didn't seem possible—not Bob, my war buddy. After living together for two years, our comradeship had strengthened into a love which for me was even greater than the feeling I had for my own brothers. We had shared everything, clothes, money, and, yes, even girls. I knew his faults and merits just as he knew mine. I cried inwardly, but I didn't break down."

"In my view, the single most important aspect of being a fighter pilot was to want to do it; to be the first to engage, and then to follow with determination. After all, this was like hunting the lion, only this time the lion could shoot back. Still, there was no greater thrill than aerial combat."
—Colonel Walker M. Mahurin, USAF (Ret), formerly with the 56th Fighter Group, Eighth USAAF

During the Korean War, Jack Bolt, a U.S. Marine Corps fighter pilot, wangled an exchange tour with the U.S. Air Force, culminating in a stint with the Oregon Air National Guard flying F-86s. Initially, however, he served in Korea with VMF-115: "I got out there about May of 1952, flying the F9F-4. I flew ninety-four missions: air-to-ground, interdictions, close air support, etc. We were down at Po Hang Do. The airfield was called K-3. That tour was coming to an end and, on taking R&R, I made contact with an Air Force squadron commander named George Ruddell. He was commanding the 39th Fighter Interceptor Squadron. I showed him I had a hundred hours, not only in the F-86 but also in the F-86F. His was the only squadron of Fs on the field, so I had experience

"'Here, Johnny. This is a bonus day. Have another drink.' I gladly accepted the offer of the free drink, but was suspicious of Mac, who didn't look into my eyes as he usually did when he handed a drink to me. His presence suddenly made me uncomfortable.

"'Somebody's got to tell you, Johnny, and I guess I'm the one. A call just came through from the RAF.

he really needed. Ruddell was friendly towards me and let me fly his birds. I just took some familiarization flights with a few guys.

"I did a second R&R trip that Christmas and, at the time, Joe McConnell, one of the leading aces in Korea with eight or nine victories, had just been grounded. Ruddell sent McConnell up to teach me some tactics. I flew two or three flights with him, and he was good. They were just fam hops; he'd had some flight infraction and Ruddell was punishing him by grounding him [from combat]. But McConnell was allowed to take test hops and teach me. I made friends with him and he really taught me a lot of things. He became the leading ace of the Korean War and was very deserving of the fame that he had. He was killed soon after the war on a test flight at Edwards Air Force Base.

"I put in for an Air Force exchange tour, so the Air Force general called the Marine general, saying, 'We're willing to have your pilots, but they come up here having never flown the plane, and they present a training burden on our people. But now we have a rare instance of having a pilot who's shown enough initiative to come up here and get checked out, and he's ready to go. Would you mind appointing John Bolt?'

"Well, there was nothing the Group could do; it came down from the Wing. They put me in Ruddell's squadron.

"McConnell became the top ace, and I was flying his on his wing when I first got up there. I was in his flight—Dog Flight—and Ruddell was really nice to me; although he was a very tough guy. He had four or five victories, but the MiGs had quit coming south of the Yalu River, and we weren't supposed to go north. If you went north of the river, it was at the risk of your professional career if you got caught. The Chinese were yelling and screaming about the 'pirates' that were coming over there, but that's where the action was. When McConnell left I took over the command of Dog Flight, a quarter of the squadron, with about twelve pilots.

"On a river-crossing flight we would take off and go full bore. We'd put those planes at 100 percent power setting until we got out of combat. They drew 100 percent all the time; engine life was planned for 800 hours and we were getting about 550 or so. Turbine blade cracks were developing. Also, we were running them at maximum temperature. You could put these little constrictors in the tailpipe—we called them 'rats'—and you could 'rat 'em up' until they ran at maximum temperature, so they were really hot rods. You'd run your drop tanks dry just about the time you got up there, and if you didn't have a contact, you weren't supposed to drop your tanks. We skinned 'em every time. By the end of the flight, on at least two occasions, I had been to over 50,000 feet in that bird. When it got empty and you still hadn't pulled power back (you were still at 100 percent), you could really get up there. The MiG-15 could get up there too.

"The 'kill rules' were, if you got seven hits on one enemy aircraft, they would give you a kill. They didn't torch off at high altitude. They simply would not burn because of the air density. So they would count the incendiary hits on them (we had good gun cameras). They figured that if you got seven hits in the fuselage, the odds were it was dead, and they'd give you a kill. They could count the incendiary hits, and they knew that every third one was an incendiary so, in effect, if you got three incendiary hits in the gun camera, they would say it was a dead MiG.

"The salvation of the F-86 was that it had good transsonic controls, and the MiG's controls were subsonic. You could cruise at about .84 Mach readily in the F-86. The MiG had to go into its uncontrollable range to attack you, and its stick forces were unmanageable. The kill ratio between the F-86 and the MiG was, to my recollection, eight to one. It was due almost exclusively to the F-86's flying tail, although there were other superior features (the gun package, for example). The MiG's gun package was meant to shoot down B-50 bombers; a 37mm and two 23mm cannons. It was overkill and not very good against fighters. Although the F-86b package was essentially the same as a World War II machine gun, the rate of fire was doubled, and it was a good gun for shooting down fighters.

"Down low, where you were out of that transsonic superiority range, we had a G suit and they didn't. You can fight defensively when you are blacked out, but you can't fight offensively. If you had enough speed to pull into a good 6G turn, you'd go black in twenty to thirty degrees of turn, and they couldn't follow you, blacked out themselves. You've lost your vision— you're still conscious, though you have three to five seconds of vision loss. When you thought you'd gone about as far as you could carry that, you could then pop the stick forward and immediately regain your vision. You'd already started your roll, and they were right there in front of you, every time, because they'd eased off in their turn. They didn't have a G-suit and your G-tolerance was twice theirs. So they were right there—they probably overshot you."

"It seemed to me that the best fighter

Pilots of the 336th fighter squadron, 4FG, in their dispersal hut at Debden.

pilots, and those who enjoyed the greater degree of success, were the ones who were quick on the uptake and had a good grasp of the tactical situation as it was developing. They were able to improvise in such a way as to gain the advantage on the enemy or, as my old boss used to say, 'turn a disadvantage into an advantage.' There are, of course, a number of other qualities that go into the matrix to make a good fighter pilot, not the least of which is luck.

"You can't fulfil the purpose of the fighter pilot, i.e. shoot down enemy planes, unless you are in the right place at the right time. Some of the other qualities which, from my observation, were possessed by the better fighter pilots were keen vision,

an unselfishness that permitted the individual to be a good team player, an inner calmness, a cool head and a steady hand. But perhaps the most critical of all was self-confidence. If you were to ask all the pilots in a squadron to name the five best pilots in the unit they would all identify the same five guys, but each would include his own name in the top five. I always thought I was one of the top two or three of the forty-five pilots in our outfit."
—Commander William E. Copeland, U.S. Navy (Ret), formerly with VF-19

In 1998, Flight Lieutenant Helen Gardiner was the only female front-line fighter pilot in the Royal Air Force. She then flew the Tornado F3 with sixteen other pilots and about sixteen

navigators of No 43 Squadron at RAF Leuchars, near St Andrews, Scotland.

For the time, Gardiner was truly unique. Yet, in an occupation where all who practice it are special, she may have been no more or less unique than any of the other pilots she was flying with on 43 Squadron. She was born in Nottingham and came to the RAF through the University Air Squadron at Newton. Other women were in the UAS with her in those days, and since then the RAF has had time to adjust to the idea of women flying fast jets—and flying them in combat. "When I was in university on the UAS, there were probably a few of the older instructors who were a little bit, 'Oooo, never in my day!' sort of attitude, but once female pilots

arrived and started going through the system, and these instructors actually saw that we could fly just as well as the next guy, they stopped getting upset about it.

"There was always the question about fast jets, front line, etc. but I think it's a case of, if you get to this stage you're obviously good enough to fly the jet or you wouldn't have got here in the first place. If you don't accept that this is the job that you do, and that you might be sent here, there, and everywhere tomorrow at the drop of a hat—then you shouldn't be here, and you probably wouldn't enjoy it anyway. I think people just accept it now quite happily.

"When I joined 43 Squadron it was a little bit daunting at first. I can't say

it wasn't. But I've been through the training system and been in the RAF long enough to know what the crew room atmosphere is like. By the time I came through the system, the instructors had seen two or three other female pilots in training. It was simply a case of 'you don't get through unless you're good enough.' Nobody came up saying 'I don't want you to be here.' There were probably some people who were a little bit wary and interested to see how I'd get on, but there were a few guys here who were instructors of mine going back through training, so they knew whether I was good enough or not. The fact that they were here, and obviously passed it on that 'she wouldn't be here unless she was good enough,' is a nice way

to arrive.

"At Leuchars, 43 Squadron then maintained two Tornado F3s and two crews on continuous Quick Reaction Alert (QRA) status, an aspect of Cold War policy. All the pilots and navigators were scheduled in a rotation for a regular twenty-four-hour QRA shift. When on QRA, the crews 'live' out on the airfield dispersal area in quarters that provide basic comforts. At each end of the building sits a HAS or hardened aircraft shelter that contained a flight-ready F3 jet, which is connected by an electric umbilical to a power source. The aircraft and crew were required to be airborne within a maximum of fifteen minutes when ordered up. " [Gardiner described a QRA assignment:] "If any Russian air-

Polish pilots flying Spitfires for the RAF.

craft decided to come round into UK airspace, we would go out and effectively escort them outside—which used to happen quite often. Now [1998] it happens very rarely, but we're still here in case anything else happens where we are required. The last time we saw any Russian aircraft come round was eighteen months ago when I actually got scrambled to go up and intercept them. We had been up a couple of days before and had been turned away at the boundary. It tends to be when there is a big naval exercise going on and it is usually their maritime patrol aircraft that come round to have a look. Obviously, with the cutbacks they've got over there, it doesn't happen that often. The second time we got airborne, they kept coming and ended up just to the north of Shetland. We actually launched both of our Q aircraft. We went up, tanked just off the North Sea, headed all the way and

intercepted them. There were two Mays [maritime patrol aircraft] and we followed them down to low level and shadowed them from behind, just keeping an eye on them. We had an E3 airborne at the time—just by chance—and we were talking to them about what the Russian aircraft were doing. We followed the Russians for about a quarter of an hour. Then our other aircraft turned up, along with our tanker which is based at Brize Norton near Oxford. We went to the tanker as we were getting short on fuel, and the other jet took over the shadowing until the Russians actually went back out of UK airspace. It was nice to be there and do a launch for real."

"The changes men have seen in this last century are hardly to be believed. It seems we exult in handing over every aspect of our lives to the idols we have created. Computers book in

our arrival and program our departure, pass our news, govern our business, and titillate our leisure. Loudspeakers shout a sermon: 'I believe in atomic fission, breaker of heaven and earth!' And as for aircraft, which in my youth, trembled like living things. If they trembled today they would be sent back to servicing for overhaul.

"We shrug and say: It can't be helped; but what captain of a transport aircraft, hedged in with courses, corridors, controls, does not long to send them all to the devil, vault into the cockpit, flip a switch and take off, bareheaded, into the wind? Perhaps not, perhaps the breed has changed—but I know which I would choose!"

When Cecil Lewis, fighter pilot and gifted writer of the Great War, wrote those words, he reflected the view of many—if not most fliers—who yearn for a simpler time and a purer flying experience.

RAF pilot transport on the base perimeter track.

Captains Duane Beeson and Don Gentile at the Debden base of the 4FG.

GALLERY

above: German Air Force pilot Horst Petzschler flew Fw 190s and Me 109s in WWII; right: RAF pilots lend a hand to move a Spitfire at its dispersal.

RAF Hurricanes landing after a wartime patrol; bottom: The remains of an RAF Eagle painting on a wall at Fowlmere; right: The famous chalk board from the White Hart pub at Brasted near the Biggin Hill base. The board contains the signatures of many prominant WWII pilots who flew from the Kent airfield.

"Lucky"

below: 56FG pilots Bob Johnson, Hub Zemke, and Bud Mahurin; left: Chief of RAF Fighter Command in WWII, Air Marshal Sir Hugh C. T. Dowding.

The Republic P-47 Thunderbolt was one of the largest, heaviest, and most powerful fighters of the Second World War. Fully loaded it could weigh up to eighth tons and could carry a bombload of 2,500 pounds. It was powered by the same Pratt & Whitney R-2800 Double Wasp engine that powered the U.S. Navy Hellcat and Corsair fighters, and was particularly effective in the ground attack role in both Europe and the Pacific.

A transport ship bringing P-47 fighters to Britain.

A cannon-armed Spitfire of No 303 (Polish)
Squadron in WWII.

below: P-51D Mustangs of the 4FG in stepped-down formation over the English countryside; right: A wartime open house day at the Lockheed Burbank P-38 Lightning assembly line, where visitors were able to view the construction of the unique fighter.

The apron area of the North American Aviation assembly plant at Inglewood, Los Angeles, California, in 1943. Mustang fighters and B-25 Mitchell bombers are lined up awaiting delivery to the U.S. Army Air Force.

left: An American P-38 fighter pilot basking in the sunshine of wartime England; below: Captain Don Gentile at his Debden base.

Polish pilots Miroslaw Feric, left and Zdzislaw Henneberg, right, with Squadron Leader Johnny Kent, of Canada.

RAF fighter pilots relaxing at dispersal with checkers and cribbage between scrambles.

left: RAF Sergeant Pilot George Unwin and friend; below: Stan Turner and his Hurricane.

In December 1942, this New Zealander poses for the camera with the latest variant of the marvelous cannon-armed Vickers-Supermarine Spitfire.

PICTURE CREDITS
Photographs by the author are credited PK. Photos from the collections of the author are credited AC. Photos from the U.S. National Archives are credited NARA. Photos by USAAF photographer Mark Brown are credited M. Brown. P3 top: Michael O'Leary, left: PK, right: M. Brown; P5: PK; P7: Cliff Knox; P9 top left: AC, bottom left: AC, top right: AC, bottom right: AC; P10 top left: AC, bottom left: PK; P11: AC; PP12-13: AC; PP14-15: RAF Museum; PP16-17: Gary Chambers; P19: AC; P20: AC; P21 both: AC; P22: PK; P23: PK; P24: PK; P26: AC; P27: USAF; P28: Bob Doe; P29 top left and right: courtesy Merle Olmsted, bottom: Imperial War Museum; P30: Imperial War Museum; P31: Bundesarchiv; P32 all: PK; P33 both: USAF; PP34-35: AC; P36: RAF Museum; P37: AC; P39: AC; PP40-41: PK; P42: AC; P44: PK; P46: Imperial War Museum; P47: AC; P48: AC; P49: AC; P50: DeGolyer Library-Southern Methodist University; PP52-53: Michael O'Leary; P55: AC; P56: PK; P57: AC; PP58-59: AC; P61: AC; P62: AC; P63: AC; P65: AC; P66: AC; P67: AC; PP68-69: Mike Durning; P70: AC; P71: Bundesarchiv; P73: Royal Navy; P75: AC; P76: AC; P77: AC; P79: Willem Honders; P80: AC; P81: NARA; P82: PK; P84: AC; PP86-93: Vickers; P95: NARA; PP96-97: AC; P98: RAF Museum; P99: AC; P100: PK; P101: PK; P102 top left: USAF, top right: PK; bottom: PK; P103: USAF; P104: AC; P106: PK; P109: courtesy Merle Olmsted; P111: M. Brown; P112: PK; P114: AC; P116: courtesy Merle Olmsted; P119: AC; P120: Cuthbert Orde; P121: AC; PP122-123: courtesy Monique Agazarian; P125: courtesy Edith Kup; P127: USAF; P129: USAF; P130: USAF; P131: courtesy Merle Olmsted; P132: courtesy Oscar Boesch; P133: USAF Museum; PP134-135: DeGolyer Library-Southern Methodist University; P136: M. Brown; P137: PK; P138: courtesy Merle Olmsted; P139: M. Brown; P140: M. Brown; P141-144: PK; P145: AC; P146: DeGolyer Library-Southern Methodist University; P147 top: AC, bottom: courtesy Merle Olmsted; P148: courtesy Quentin Bland; P149: PK; PP150-151: USAF Academy Library; PP152-153: AC; P154: AC; P155: AC; P156: USAF Museum; P157: AC; P158: Michael Brazier; PP160-161: all M. Brown; PP162-169 all: courtesy Mary Lou Colbert Neale and Jack Ilfrey; P170: AC; P173: courtesy Andy Saunders; P174: AC; PP176-177 both: DeGolyer Library-Southern Methodist University; P179: Edward Reeves; P180: USAF Academy Library; P182 both: AC; P183: courtesy Jack Ilfrey; PP184-185: courtesy Andy Saunders; PP186-187: AC; P188: AC; P191: Imperial War Museum; PP192-193: M. Brown; P194: AC; PP196-197: AC; P198: RAF Museum; P200: DeGolyer Library-Southern Methodist University; P201-209: AC; P210: courtesy Horst Petzschler; P211: AC; P212 top: AC, bottom: PK; P213: AC; P214: AC; P215: M. Brown; PP216-217: Fairchild Republic Company; PP218-219: AC; PP220-221: AC; P222: DeGolyer Library-Southern Methodist University; PP223-225: AC; P226: USAF; P227: AC; PP228-232: AC; P233: Imperial War Museum; PP234-235: AC. P237: John Burgess; P240: AC.

ACKNOWLEDGMENTS
The author is grateful to the following for their generous help in the development of this book: Monique Agazarian, Malcolm Bates, Paddy Barthropp, George Behling, Nick Berryman, Robert Best, Donald Blakeslee, Quentin Bland, Oscar Boesch, John Bolt, Michael Brazier, Bob Brown, Eric Brown, Mark Brown, Kazimierz Budzik, Piers Burnett, Shimon Camiel, John Carroll, James Cain, Gary Chambers, George Chandler, Kim Chetwyn, Albert P. Clark, Evelyn Clarke, Pat and Richard Collier, Ed Copeland, Kate and Jack Currie, Robert Floyd Cooper, John Cunnick, Randy "Duke" Cunningham, Al Deere, Bob Doe, Dale Donovan, James H. Doolittle, Glenn Duncan, Gary Dunlop, Dewey Durnford, Frantisek Fajtl, Lou Fleming, Christopher Foxley-Norris, Betty Frey, Royal Frey, Ella and Oz Freire, Adolf Galland, William Ganz, Helen Gardiner, Geoffrey Goodman, James Goodson, Jim Gray, Stephen Grey, Peter Grosserhode, Grover C. Hall, Roger Hall, Mark Hanna, Ray Hanna, Mike Herrling, Bill Hess, Jonathan Holdaway, Willem Honders, Jack Ilfrey, Markus Isphoding, Yasuho Izawa, Hans Joachim Jabs, Hargi Kaplan, Margaret Kaplan, Neal Kaplan, Cliff Knox, Walter Konantz, Edith Kup, James Kyle, John Lamb, Charles Lawson, Alan Leahy, Robert Littlefield, Gidi Livni, Grant Lucas, Harvey Mace, Walker M. Mahurin, Richard May, Judy McCutcheon, Rick McCutcheon, Carroll McColpin, Bert McDowell, Tilly McMaster, John McQuarrie, Hamilton McWhorter, Tony Mead, Sandra Merrill, H. Moranville, May Lou Colbert Neale, John Nesbitt-Duffort, Leo Nomis, William O'Brien, Michael O'Leary, Merle Olmsted, William Overstreet, Geoffrey Page, Frantisek Perina, Horst Petzschler, John Phegley, Steve Pisanos, Günther Rall, Duane Reed, Paul Riley, Art Roscoe, Andy Saunders, Robert L. Scott, Eudora Seyfer, William Sharpe, E.A.W. Smith, David Soper, Lloyd Stovall, Gitte Sturm, Stephan Stritter, Robert Strobell, Anne and Dickie Turley-George, Peter Townsend, Stanley Vejtasa, Bill Vincent, David Wade, Ray Wagner, Douglas Warren, Edward Wendorf, Dirk Wiegmann, Frank Wootton, Denis Wissler, Dennis Wrynn, Jan Zdarsky, Hub Zemke.

Grateful acknowledgment is made to the following for permission to reprint their previously publsihed material: Eric Brown for excerpts from Wings of the Luftwaffe and Wings of the Navy; Harper Collins for excerpt from One of the Few by J. A. Kent; Randy Cunningham for excerpt from Fox Two, published by Warner Books, reprinted by permission; James H. Farmer for excerpts from Celluloid Wings, published by Tab Books; Greenhill Books for excerpts from Sagittarius Rising by Cecil Lewis, reprinted by permission of Greenhill Books on behalf of Fanny Lewis; Roger Hall for excerpt from Clouds of Fear, published by Coronet Books; Robert M. Littlefield for excerpts from Double Nickel–Double Trouble, published by R. M. Littlefield. Reprinted by permission; Macmillan General Books for excerpts from The Last Enemy by Richard Hillary. Reprinted by Permission; Walker M. Mahurin for excerpts from Honest John, published by G.P. Putnam's Sons. Reprinted by permission; Sandra Merrill for excerpts from Donald's Story, published by Tebidine. Reprinted by permission; John Nesbitt-Duffort for excerpt from Scramble, published by Speed and Sports Publications Ltd; W.W. Norton Company for excerpts from Serenade to the Big Bird, by Bert Stiles; Geoffrey Page for excerpt from Tale of a Guinea Pig, published by Corgi; Penguin Books Ltd for excerpts from Team Tornado by John Peters and John Nichol, copyright © 1994 by the authors; Random House for excerpts from The Look of Eagles by John T. Godfrey, copyright renewed 1986 by Robert E.. Godfrey and John T. Godfrey. Reprinted by permission of Random House, Inc; Eudora Seyfer for Remembering Raydon, published by Mature Outlook magazine; Vintage-Random House for excerpt from The Fatal Englishman by Sebastian Faulks. Reprinted by permission; Wind Canyon Publishing, Inc. for "Dogfight Over Paris," by Henry C. Woodrum. Reprinted by permission. All reasonable efforts have been made to contact those believed to hold copyright for previously published material reprinted in Lone Eagle. We apologize for any inconvenience caused to copyright holders whom we have been unable to contact.

BIBLIOGRAPHY
American Fighter Aces Association, American Fighter Aces Album, 1978.
Barker, A. J., The Yom Kippur War, Ballantine Books, 1974.
Bekker, Cajus, The Luftwaffe War Diaries, Doubleday & Co., Inc., 1968.
Brown, Eric, Wings of the Luftwaffe, Airlife Publishing Ltd., 1993
Bishop, Edward, The Battle of Britain, George Allen and Unwin Ltd., 1960.
Brown, Eric, Wings of the Navy, Airlife Publishing Ltd, 1987.
Clancy, Tom, Fighter Wing, Berkley Books, 1995.
Collier, Richard, Eagle Day, Pan Books, 1968.
Costello, John, Love, Sex & War, Collins, 1985.
Deere, Alan, Nine Lives, Hodder & Stoughton, 1959.
Farmer, James H., Celluloid Wings, Tab Books, 1984.

Faulks, Sebastian, *The Fatal Englishman*, Vintage, 1997.

Freeman, Roger, *Mighty Eighth War Diary*, Jane's, 1981.

Galland, Adolf, *The First and the Last*, Ballantine Books, 1954.

Gallico, Paul, *The Hurricane Story*, Four Square Books, 1967.

Gurney, Gene, *Five Down and Glory*, Ballantine Books, 1958.

Hall, Grover C., *1000 Destroyed*, Putnam, 1946.

Hall, Roger, *Clouds of Fear*, Coronet Books, 1975.

Haugland, Vern, *The Eagle Squadrons*, Ziff-Davis Flying Books, 1979.

Hillary, Richard, *The Last Enemy*, Macmillan & Co., Ltd., 1950.

Ilfrey, Jack, with Reynolds, Max, *Happy Jack's Go-Buggy*, Exposition Press, 1979.

Infield, Glenn, *Big Week*, Pinnacle Books, 1974.

Kent, J. A., *One of the Few*, Corgi, 1975.

Lewis, Cecil, *Sagittarius Rising*, Greenhill Books, 1993.

Littlefield, Robert, *Double Nickel–Double Trouble*, R. M. Littlefield, 1993.

Lloyd, Ian, *Rolls-Royce: The Merlin at War*, Macmillan Press Ltd., 1978.

Mahurin, Walker M., *Honest John*, G.P. Putnam's Sons, 1962.

Merrill, Sandra, *Donald's Story*, Tebidine, 1996.

O'Leary, Michael, *Mustang: A Living Legend*, Osprey, 1987.

Olmsted, Merle, *The 357th Over Europe*, Phalanx, 1994.

Olmsted, Merle, *The Yoxford Boys*, Aero Publishers Inc., 1971.

Page, Geoffrey, *Tale of a Guinea Pig*, Wingham Press, 1991.

Peters, John and Nichol, John, *Team Tornado*, Penguin Group, 1994.

Quill, Jeffrey, *Spitfire*, Arrow Books, 1985.

Robinson, Derek, *Piece of Cake*, Alfred A. Knopf, 1984.

Sakai, Saburo, with Caidin, Martin, and Saito, Fred, *Samurai*, Four Square Books, 1966.

Scutts, Jerry, *Fighter Operations*, Patrick Stephens Ltd., 1992.

Speer, Frank, *Wingman*, Frank Speer, 1993.

Toliver, Raymond F. and Constable, Trevor J., *Fighter Aces*, The Macmillan Company, 1965.

Townsend, Peter, *Duel of Eagles*, Simon and Schuster, 1970.

Turner, Richard, *Mustang Pilot*, New English Library, 1975.

Wagner, Ray, *Mustang Designer*, Orion Books, 1990.

Wagner, Ray, *The North American Sabre*, Doubleday and Company, 1963.

Willis, John, *Churchill's Few*, Michael Joseph, 1985.

Yeager, Chuck and Janos, Leo, *Yeager*, Bantam Books, 1985.

Zemke, Hub, with Freeman, Roger A., *Zemke's Wolf Pack*, Orion Books, 1988.

Sergeant Pilot John Burgess.

INDEX